Tana's
kitchen secrets

Tana's
kitchen secrets

MITCHELL BEAZLEY

Contents

Introduction 6

Kitchen kit secrets 8

Pantry secrets 11

Slow & easy meat 12

Quick & easy meat 42

Fish 68

Pasta, rice, & grains 100

Pies, pastries, tarts, & batters 120

Vegetables 152

A bit of dough 190

Something sweet 204

Cakes & cookies 240

Sauces & dressings 268

Index 284

Thanks 288

Introduction

I want this book to help you to love cooking. I've written it for people who enjoy food but who, like me, suddenly find they needed to expand their recipe repertoire and their cooking skills—either because they have a family to feed or for some other reason. I now cook a variety of dishes every day. My four kids always have a homemade meal after school, and then I make something for Gordon and me later in the evening. And I love to plan weekends filled with nurturing, delicious food that we can all share.

I cook because I want to be confident about what my family eats. I want to feel sure that the meat is good, or that the bread is wholesome and nutritious. Our kids know what fresh food tastes like and I am glad this is the norm for them, not something they'll have to learn. I want your children to be the same.

With a busy life, I don't have hours to spend shopping, prepping, and planning dinner. Quite often, food is bought on the way home and meals are made in the minimum of time…but I want maximum results. These recipes will help you to achieve that, too.

Don't be scared to teach yourself to cook—I did! Use my recipes as a guideline: if you can't find an ingredient, don't panic. When I was making my Haddock & Spring Vegetable Risotto (*see* page 112), I didn't have the parsley I was going to use, so I added mint…and it was much better! Always add your favorite ingredients and leave out anything you're not so keen on. The only rule is to taste all the time, so you'll know when you're on the right road.

Remember that your family needs a balanced diet. I always try to remind myself to eat as much fish as I do meat and sometimes (much to Gordon's horror) sneak in a vegetarian day!

We have a good butcher and fish market but, if you're not so lucky, don't worry. I also buy meat from a supermarket that employs a proper butcher. Always talk to the person behind the counter when you've found someone you trust. They can tell you what cut of meat to choose and how to cook it, or what fish to use for fish cakes (*see* pages 88–9) when it needs to taste great but it doesn't matter what it looks like. Let them advise you, because they know what they are doing. And they can save you money, too.

Every family needs time around the table. The best times are when all six of us are together. When you sit down as a family, you hear about who got a good grade on a test, or who got onto the lacrosse team. We've got to stay close to our kids so they can tell us these things, and around the table is the perfect place. This book will help you make those wonderful family meals, so enjoy it!

Kitchen kit secrets

Here are some of what I consider to be the essential pieces of equipment that you should have in your kitchen.

Pans Every cook needs a selection of pans with lids. They must be dishwasher-proof and nonstick—especially for scrambled eggs, unless you love washing up! It's handy to have an ovenproof pan, so you can transfer a piece of meat or fish directly from the stovetop to the oven.

Knives and sharpeners The sharper the knives, the less likely you are to cut yourself, however weird that may sound. So you must have a knife sharpener.

Microplane grater Fantastic for grating everything from citrus zest to Parmesan. My favorite broke recently after a very long life and I was heartbroken.

Cheese shaver To make neat slices for sandwiches.

Food processor For easy curry pastes. To save time, I also use it to chop onions. It makes sauces so much easier and less time-consuming.

Strainers Have a tiny strainer—or even a tea strainer—for dusting the top of cakes and tarts (*see* page 138), for instant prettification.

Scissors You'll need a good strong pair of these, hidden somewhere so they can't be stolen by the kids and end up getting covered in glitter and glue!

Mixing bowls I love glass. Gordon likes stainless-steel bowls, but they always remind me of dog bowls. So he has his cupboard with his bowls and I have mine with my glass.

Plastic spatulas I have three spatulas—small, medium, and large—and I am rather obsessive about them.

Cake pans I love loaf pans for banana loaves or Cherry & Almond Loaf (*see* page 248), which I make frequently. I also have a couple of round cake pans, and muffin pans.

Cookie cutters I'm a bit like a child in a toy shop when I see these—you can never have too many shapes!

Digital kitchen scales Essential.

Oven mitts Don't use dish cloths to move hot dishes and baking sheets as it's far easier to burn yourself. Use mitts, preferably a pair that cover your skin up to the elbows.

Kitchen towels Always place a kitchen towel under your chopping board so it doesn't slip. This will save your fingers from many nicks.

Small chopping board These are great for those times when you want to chop only a small amount of something. Mine is used regularly for the lemons and limes for our evening gin and tonic.

Large chopping board I use wooden chopping boards as platters for cold meats and cheese: they look so attractive.

Olive oil The very best thing for wooden surfaces around your kitchen sink, and for chopping boards. It's protective and prevents mold and warping.

Pantry secrets

Below are some tips on what food items you should have in your pantry at all times so that you are always prepared to whip up a quick, tasty meal.

Stock up your larder Don't feel daunted by the length of this list: you can collect things a little at a time. Make sure you have some chutneys, tomato puree, canned tomatoes, coconut milk, and sweet corn. I keep Worcestershire sauce, ketchup, steak sauce, and grainy mustard. Make sure you have baking powder, self-rising and all-purpose flours, and superfine and granulated sugars for baking, as well as dried yeast and vanilla extract (beans if you're feeling flush). You'll need basmati, risotto and brown rices, couscous, lentils, and dried pasta shapes with a jar of pesto. I wouldn't be without miso paste, and it's handy to have Thai red curry paste for shrimp (*see* page 92) and Thai green curry paste for chicken. Hoisin and soy sauces, white and red wine vinegars will lift the flavor of many sauces. Lastly, always have a jar of honey.

Refrigerator Start your weekend with a full refrigerator. We have salad, cheese (always a nice block of Parmesan), ham and chorizo, marinated artichokes, anchovies and peppers, fresh pasta, low-fat crème fraîche, pancetta, fresh vine tomatoes, free-range eggs, and fresh vegetables. And a beautiful free-range chicken. So there's always something to eat, even if it's just scrambled eggs. Our daughter Megan makes the best, finishing them with crème fraîche to stop them from overcooking.

Get ahead Try to have cookie doughs in the refrigerator, rolled into sausage shapes and wrapped in plastic wrap so you can instantly bake—the house will smell delicious. That aroma has the same effect on me as piles of clean, fluffy laundry—it's so comforting!

The vegetable rack Have chiles, garlic, and onions, ready for all sorts of sauces.

Freezer I always have Frozen Fruit (*see* page 221), frozen peas, and sweet corn. If I have a busy week ahead, I'll freeze a pot of Chicken Cacciatore (*see* page 34) to have an emergency meal in hand.

Spices Keep spices in a dark cupboard to preserve their flavor. I use sea salt flakes and both white and black peppercorns, chili powder and garam masala, ground cumin, coriander, and cinnamon, star anise, cinnamon sticks, and cloves. Buy kaffir lime leaves and curry leaves in bulk from Asian markets— they freeze wonderfully.

Hot sauce We go through a lot of this and it all goes into our son Jack! He even puts a bottle in his pocket in case there's none where he's going! Although you won't have Jack, there's always someone who wants to put hot sauce on everything, so it's good to have a bottle handy.

Oil You'll need mild vegetable and olive oils for everyday cooking, and a bottle of good stuff for drizzling over salads and fish. Never cook with expensive olive oil, as the precious aromas are destroyed by heat.

Sprinkles I collect these in all kinds of colors and shapes, and have some great multicolored dinosaurs at the moment! There are always school bake sales and it can get competitive with other moms…you need to stay ahead of the game!

Slow & easy meat

Really rustic shoulder of lamb · Shepherd's pie
Lauren's meatballs · Crackling roast pork · Spicy beef stew
Parmesan chicken drumsticks · Chicken cacciatore · Chicken broth
Poached whole chicken · Roasted guinea fowl with lemon & garlic

Secrets of slow & easy meat

When you slow cook, you can choose the cheaper cuts, such as shoulder of lamb or chuck roast, that need time in the oven for the sinews to tenderize. And the slower you cook them, the more they relax. Not only does this free you up from the stove while it putters away, but it also fills your home with a delicious aroma. Your family will know that dinner is going to be wonderful.

If you have a young family, these recipes are ideal. Because they are very forgiving and don't need exact timing, you won't have to cook twice, once for the kids and once for yourself. You can put a recipe such as my Chicken Cacciatore (*see* page 34) in the oven while the children are doing their homework. Then they can eat early and you can leave the pot on a very low heat so that, like Gordon and me, the grown-ups can eat it later.

It's easy to turn slow-cooked dishes into other meals, which is excellent news if, as I do, you hate waste. When I make Really Rustic Shoulder of Lamb (*see* page 16), I turn the leftover flaked meat into a curry for the kids, adding vegetables, garam masala, cumin, mango chutney, and yogurt.

Every week you should cook a meal with ground meat… I love it! It's so versatile. Always make sure you buy freshly ground meat from a quality source. I start off with a basic bolognese for the children, then Gordon and I spice it up into chili con carne for our meal, with some judicious seasonings. Ground meat reheats and freezes like a dream. It's my standby dish.

When I was growing up we had a roast every Sunday, though we have it only once or twice a month now. You'll need a day when you have an hour to see to it, so choose a bleak, chilly afternoon. It's important to have decent family time together, and my Crackling Roast Pork (*see* page 27) makes a wonderful, warming, winter family meal.

In this chapter you'll find the best recipe to have up your sleeve when you need a dish for a carry-in supper or picnic. My Poached Whole Chicken (*see* page 38) is incredibly easy. It must be served at room temperature, so lends itself brilliantly to picnic hampers. Never serve it chilled; I hate "fridge-cold" food. Take it to the picnic and eat with a generous helping of Tomato & Tarragon Mayonnaise (*see* page 272) and New Potato Salad (*see* page 188).

Really rustic shoulder of lamb

This is one of the cheapest cuts of lamb available and is suitable for a succulent slow roast as it has lots of hard-working fibers that break down over a long cooking time. The richer-tasting mutton would be excellent for this recipe as well.

Serves 4
Preparation time 5–10 minutes
Cooking time 3 hours 30 minutes

4lb square-cut shoulder roast of lamb
   (bone in)
1 tsp dried thyme
1 tsp dried marjoram
1 tsp coriander seeds
1 tsp ground cinnamon
sea salt and black pepper
3 tbsp olive oil
2 rosemary sprigs

1 Preheat the oven to 400°F.

2 Pat the lamb dry with paper towels (*see* secret, page 27). Using a small, sharp knife, make slits all over the shoulder, each about 1in long. Grind together all the dried herbs and spices in a mortar and pestle until you have a powder. Season with salt and pepper, add the oil, and mix to a paste. Rub it all over the lamb shoulder and down into all the slits.

3 Place the lamb and rosemary into a roasting dish and put in the oven for 25–30 minutes, until nicely browned. Take the lamb out of the oven and cover with foil, sealing tightly around the edges. Reduce the oven to 325°F and return the meat to the oven for 3 hours, until it can be easily pulled apart with a fork.

4 Remove the roast from the oven and allow it to rest for 10 minutes, then pull the meat off the bone. Mix it with the juices in the roasting dish. Serve on a platter on the table for everyone to help themselves.

Choosing the right lamb

Meat from a young lamb will look pink, while the meat of an older animal should be reddish in hue. A spring lamb is 3–5 months old, and a lamb is under 1 year. A yearling is 12–24 months, whereas the richer-tasting mutton, which is less widely available but would be excellent for this recipe, is more than 2 years of age.

Shepherd's pie

Over the years I have made my mom's version of this dish, my mother-in-law's recipe, and invented my own too, gradually adding more ingredients and trying to modernize it. However, this is a very traditional pie, and less is more in this case. It's great served with peas.

Serves 6–8
Preparation time 20 minutes
Cooking time 40 minutes
Can be made in advance
Suitable for freezing

2 tbsp olive oil
2lb 4oz ground lamb
sea salt and black pepper
2 tbsp tomato puree
1 large onion, finely chopped
1 garlic clove, finely chopped
3 carrots, finely chopped
1 celery stalk, finely chopped
leaves from 2 rosemary sprigs, finely chopped
1½ tbsp instant gravy mix
2 tbsp steak sauce
Worcestershire sauce

For the topping
5lb Yukon Gold potatoes
large knob of butter (about 2 tbsp)
splash of milk
2 egg yolks

Perfect mashed potatoes

Your cooked potatoes should be as dry as possible, to avoid a horrid watery mash. After draining, return them to the pan over low heat for a few minutes, watching so they don't scorch, until all the steam has been driven off. Try adding sweet potato, parsnip, or celeriac for delicious variations, but always include potato for smoothness. Then, of course, mash in generous amounts of butter and milk, cream, or sour cream.

1 Pour half the oil into a skillet over medium heat, add the lamb and season with salt and pepper. Turn and break up the meat with a wooden spoon and allow it to brown all over; keep stirring or it might burn. Tip it into a colander to drain off the fat.

2 Add the remaining oil to the skillet over a medium heat and return the lamb to the pan. Add the tomato puree and stir to coat for 1–2 minutes, then mix in the onion, garlic, carrots, celery, and rosemary. Season again, stir and allow the vegetables to soften.

3 Dissolve the gravy mix in 2 cups boiling water, then add it to the pan with the steak sauce. Let the liquid simmer gently and reduce slightly, then stir in the Worcestershire sauce. Leave to simmer gently for 20 minutes. Preheat the oven to 400°F.

4 Meanwhile, make the topping. Cut the potatoes into even-size pieces and put them in a saucepan. Add enough cold water to cover and a good pinch of salt, then bring to a boil over high heat. Reduce the heat and simmer for 15 minutes, or until tender. Drain well (*see* secret, left) and mash with the butter and milk, season, then add the egg yolks (to help the topping brown well) and stir rapidly.

5 Place the lamb into an 8½-cup ovenproof dish and cover with the mash. Fork the top gently to ensure a lovely crunchy topping. Cook in the oven for 20 minutes, until bubbling gently and golden brown with lovely crispy bits.

Lauren's meatballs

Lauren is a totally self-taught cook who has worked for Gordon for a couple of years. I was moaning to her that I wanted to cook more meatballs and she gave me this fabulous recipe. She has an amazing ability to put flavors together in an easy and inspiring way.

Serves 4
Preparation time 20 minutes
Cooking time 40–45 minutes
Can be made in advance to end of step 4

1 tbsp olive oil, plus extra for the baking sheet
1in fresh ginger, peeled and finely chopped
2 garlic cloves, crushed
1 large onion, finely sliced
1 eggplant, cut into ½in dice
3 tbsp medium-hot curry paste
13.5oz can coconut milk
1 cup chicken stock
sea salt and black pepper
juice of ½ lime (about 1 tbsp)

For the meatballs
1lb 2oz ground lamb
large handful of flatleaf parsley leaves,
    roughly chopped
small handful of mint leaves,
    roughly chopped
1 egg yolk
2 tbsp tomato puree

Shaping meatballs, burgers, and koftas

When shaping ground meat into meatballs, burgers, or Middle Eastern-style koftas, always have a bowl of cold water handy. Wet your hands before shaping and rolling the meat into equal-size balls. This helps to make the mixture pliable and stops it sticking to your hands. Chill the shaped meat before cooking to firm it up, making the meatballs, burgers, or koftas less likely to fall apart.

1 To make the sauce, heat the oil in a large non-stick skillet over medium heat, add the ginger, garlic, and onion and stir for 10 minutes, or until softened and translucent but not browned. Add the eggplant and continue to cook for 5–10 minutes until soft. Stir in the curry paste, then add the coconut milk and stock. Bring to a simmer, season with salt and pepper and cook for 25–30 minutes.

2 For the meatballs, place the ground lamb into a mixing bowl and add the chopped herbs and egg yolk, stir in the tomato puree, season with salt and pepper, and mix until everything is evenly combined. Roll the mixture into 16 small balls (*see* secret, below left), put them on a plate, cover, and place in the refrigerator for 20 minutes to firm up. Preheat the oven to 425°F.

3 Place the meatballs onto an oiled baking sheet and cook for 10–15 minutes, turning once halfway through, until nicely browned all over.

4 Meanwhile, pour the sauce into a blender and process until smooth. You may have to do this in batches as the blender should be no more than half full each time to avoid splashing; hold the lid on with a kitchen towel to protect your hands from the hot liquid. Pour the pureed sauce into a large saucepan and carefully add the meatballs.

5 Simmer gently for 20 minutes. Taste, adjust the seasoning and stir in the lime juice to brighten the flavor. These are great served on a bed of steamed basmati rice.

Crackling roast pork

This is a great traditional Sunday roast and so simple to do. Have it with some roasted vegetables; you'll find plenty of recipes in the Vegetables chapter (see pages 152–89). Don't be worried about making the skin crispy; the easy tips here work a treat.

Serves 4
Preparation time 10 minutes
Cooking time 1 hour 20 minutes,
   plus 30 minutes resting

2lb 4oz boneless pork leg roast
   (fresh ham), rind scored
1–2 tbsp sea salt
black pepper
4 tbsp olive oil

1 Preheat the oven to 425°F. You need this blast of heat to sear the meat and give the crisp skin (crackling) a good head start.

2 Dry the meat (*see* secret, below left). Score the fat diagonally at 1in intervals, first in one direction, then in the other, to produce a diamond pattern. Rub the salt all over the fat, getting well into the scored slits, season with pepper, and drizzle with oil. Cook in a roasting dish for 30 minutes, or until the crackling is blistered and golden.

3 Turn the oven down to 325°F and cook the pork for another 50 minutes. To check it is cooked through, slide a knife into the center of the joint, leave for 10 seconds, then remove and touch the tip to the inside of your arm where it is sensitive to heat. If it's really hot, the pork is cooked. The juices should run clear with no trace of pink.

4 Turn off the oven and leave the pork inside to rest for 20 minutes, then remove and rest for 10 minutes more at room temperature. Meanwhile, skim the fat from the juices and put them into a small pan over high heat to reduce to an intense, thin gravy.

5 Serve the pork with the gravy and my Chunky Apple Sauce (*see* page 280) and accompany with roasted carrots and parsnips.

Preparing meat for roasting

With this or any other roast of red meat, a good habit to get into is to let it air-dry before roasting. It will give pork better crackling, while lamb and beef will become crisp at the edges. Pat the meat as dry as possible with paper towels, then leave the joint, uncovered, at room temperature for an hour—or overnight in the refrigerator—to allow the remaining moisture to evaporate.

Spicy beef stew

This is a quick, one-pot dish that you can leave slow-cooking in the oven. The long cooking time allows the spices to develop a wonderfully rounded flavor. This is a great dish from the pantry, needing very few fresh ingredients. Serve with lots of fluffy white rice.

Serves 4
Preparation time 10 minutes
Cooking time 1 hour 45 minutes
Can be made in advance
Suitable for freezing

1lb 2oz chuck roast, cut into 1in dice
sea salt
2 tsp garam masala
1 tsp chili powder
1 tbsp all-purpose flour
4 tbsp vegetable oil
4 carrots, cut into 1in dice
2 tbsp tomato puree
4 star anise
1 cinnamon stick
1 dried chile, finely chopped
2 × 14.5oz cans chopped tomatoes
2 bay leaves
black pepper

1 Preheat the oven to 350°F. Place the steak into a large mixing bowl with a good pinch of salt, the garam masala, chili powder, and flour. Mix so all the beef is coated.

2 Pour 3 tbsp of the oil into a large flameproof casserole over medium-high heat. When the oil is simmering, add the beef and cook, turning, until all sides have a good color (*see* secret, below). Place a colander over a bowl and pour in the beef to allow excess fat to drain off.

3 Add the remaining oil to the casserole, add the carrots and allow them to color slightly, stirring so they do not stick or burn. Return the meat to the casserole and add the tomato puree. Stir for 2–3 minutes so the puree is cooked through. Toss in the star anise, cinnamon, dried chile, tomatoes, bay leaves, and 1 cup boiling water. Season well with salt and pepper and cover.

4 Transfer the casserole to the oven and cook for 1 hour 30 minutes. Check it every now and then—if the stew seems to be thickening too much, add a little more boiling water. At the end of cooking, turn off the oven, open the door slightly and let the dish cool for 10–20 minutes. The beef should be lovely and tender with a good kick of spice.

Browning meat for stewing

The trick to an excellent casseroled dish is to brown the meat very well before stewing slowly. You will usually have to do so in batches as, if a pan is overcrowded, the meat will steam and never take on a good caramelized color. Fry your chosen meat, turning occasionally, until all sides are dark gold, to bring out a wonderfully savory, roasted taste along with an inherent sweetness.

Parmesan chicken drumsticks

Try this delicious recipe with other cuts of chicken such as tenders or thighs, but remember that the boneless tenders will need far less time in the oven to cook through; start checking them after 10–15 minutes and don't leave them in for too long or they will dry out.

Serves 4
Preparation time 5 minutes
Cooking time 35–40 minutes
Can be made in advance to end of step 3
Suitable for freezing at end of step 3

3 tbsp butter
1 tbsp olive oil, plus extra for the
   baking sheet
16 chicken drumsticks
1 cup finely grated Parmesan cheese
2 tbsp dried oregano
2 tbsp paprika
2 tsp dried parsley
sea salt and black pepper
crisp, green salad, to serve

1 Preheat the oven to 375°F.

2 Melt the butter in a saucepan over low heat, then add the oil. Pour into a mixing bowl, add the chicken, and turn to coat the drumsticks evenly.

3 Mix together the Parmesan, oregano, paprika, and parsley in another bowl and season well with salt and pepper. Drop each buttered drumstick into the mixture, turning until all sides are well coated and pressing the meat well to make sure the coating sticks. (Alternatively, *see* secret, below.) At this point you can cover and refrigerate the drumsticks for a few hours until ready to use (this often helps the coating to adhere), but bring them back to room temperature before cooking.

4 Place the drumsticks on a lightly oiled baking sheet. Bake for 35 minutes, until golden and crispy, turning once halfway through cooking. To check they are cooked, insert a small, sharp knife or skewer into the thickest part of the drumstick, piercing right to the bone, then remove. The juices that come out should run clear; if there is any trace of pink, return the drumsticks to the oven for 5 minutes, then test again.

5 Serve with a crisp, green salad.

Applying coatings to meat

To save on dishwashing, add the coating ingredients into a large resealable plastic bag and shake to combine. Add the meat, seal the bag and shake it well until the meat is evenly coated. Massage the meat through the bag to press the coating on firmly.

Chicken cacciatore

This recipe is not at all like the classic dish with the same title, but the name has stuck in our home! It is a really quick and easy supper requiring minimum effort. I usually serve it with buttered baked potatoes. You can use 2lb 4oz of very ripe fresh tomatoes instead of canned if you prefer.

Serves 4 hungry children, with seconds
Preparation time 15–20 minutes
Cooking time 1 hour 15 minutes
Can be made in advance to end of step 5
Suitable for freezing at end of step 5

2 tbsp olive oil
1 onion, finely chopped
2 garlic cloves, finely chopped
sea salt and black pepper
2 tbsp finely chopped rosemary leaves
6 canned anchovies, roughly chopped
1 tbsp tomato puree
3 × 14.5oz cans chopped tomatoes
handful of fresh parsley leaves,
    finely chopped
6 free-range chicken legs

Which cut to choose?

Chicken legs are ideal for this dish. Choose plump pieces with undamaged skin. Legs are cheap and have the dark meat that is best for casseroles and other slow-cooked dishes as it remains moist, whereas chicken breasts will soon dry out. Breasts should be reserved for quicker cooking to keep them juicy and succulent. You could also try making this and other slow-cooked recipes with inexpensive chicken wings, though they will cook more quickly than legs (start checking for doneness after 25 minutes).

1 Preheat the oven to 375°F.

2 Pour 1 tbsp of the oil into a deep skillet and place over medium heat. Add the onion and garlic, and a pinch of salt, and cook for 10 minutes, or until softened but not browned. Add the rosemary and anchovies, allowing the anchovies to break up and almost melt into the onions and garlic. Stir in the tomato puree.

3 Add the canned tomatoes (or fresh if you have the patience to peel them!), season well with salt and pepper to taste, and simmer for 10–15 minutes until the sauce begins to thicken. Stir in half the parsley.

4 Meanwhile, heat the remaining oil in a separate skillet over medium heat and brown the chicken legs on all sides. As well as making the chicken crispy, this will render and remove a fair amount of the fat.

5 Using a slotted spoon, remove the chicken legs from the pan and place in an ovenproof dish with a close-fitting lid. Pour the tomato sauce over the top and put the lid on. Bake for 40 minutes, or until cooked through. To check it is ready, pierce the thickest part of a chicken leg with a small, sharp knife, right down to the bone, then remove. If the juices run clear, it is ready. If there is even a trace of pink, return to the oven for 5 minutes, then test again.

6 Sprinkle over the remaining parsley before serving.

Chicken broth

I give this restorative, calming soup to the kids when they come home late from swimming. Add any vegetables that you want, such as crunchy green beans, peapods, broccoli florets, sugarsnap peas, and baby sweet corn. You can also choose to keep the broth plain, without vegetables or cream. Kaffir lime leaves can be found dried, and sometimes fresh, in Asian markets.

Serves 4 as a starter
Preparation time 5–10 minutes
Cooking time 2 hours
Can be made in advance
Suitable for freezing

8 free-range chicken legs
1 large onion, cut into wedges
2 carrots, cut into 1in chunks
1 leek, roughly chopped
¾in fresh ginger, peeled, and
   roughly chopped
2 bay leaves
2 kaffir lime leaves
small handful of lemon thyme sprigs
2 stems of lemon grass, crushed
2 tsp coriander seeds
1 tsp white peppercorns
2 star anise
sea salt and black pepper
1 cup selected vegetables, chopped
   (*see* recipe introduction)
²/₃ cup heavy cream (optional)

1 Place the chicken legs into a stock pot or large saucepan. Pour in 7 cups cold water, or enough to cover. Bring to a boil over low heat, skim off any scum that rises to the surface, then add all the other ingredients except the selected vegetables and the cream. Keep on a very low simmer for about 2 hours, skimming any scum, and adding water when necessary to keep the ingredients covered.

2 Add your vegetables and simmer gently until crisp but tender (about 5 minutes, depending on which vegetables you choose) and stir in some cream, if you like. Strain through a large fine-mesh strainer into a bowl, reserving any chicken meat you may want to shred into the broth. Season to taste with salt and pepper and serve piping hot.

Making your own stock

Homemade stock is a great way to use up cooked chicken bones and carcasses (the legs used here give a richer taste). Naturally, use beef bones instead for beef stock, and so on. Always cover the bones with cold water; as the water comes to a boil, the fat comes to the surface, at which point you can skim it off. Add any flavorings that you like, remembering that onions and carrots give a delicate sweetness. Skim to remove impurities and prevent cloudiness. Use at once, or freeze.

Poached whole chicken

This is a great item to have in the refrigerator for packed lunches, picnics, or salads as the chicken stays lovely and moist throughout. If you are using it in a salad, add new potatoes, warm asparagus, or my Tomato & Tarragon Mayonnaise (see page 272).

Serves 4
Preparation time 5–10 minutes
Cooking time 1 hour 40 minutes
Can be made in advance

1 whole chicken (about 3–4lb), preferably free range
1 tbsp coriander seeds
1 tbsp white peppercorns
3 bay leaves
4 rosemary sprigs
1 tbsp sea salt
4 garlic cloves
1 celery stalk, roughly chopped
1 carrot, halved
1 onion, quartered

1 Place the chicken in a very large pot. Fill with enough cold water just to cover, then add all the other ingredients.

2 Bring to a boil over medium heat, then reduce the heat to the lowest possible setting, cover and simmer very gently for 1 hour 30 minutes, until you can easily remove a chicken leg from the body. Allow to cool a little in the stock and skim the top if necessary.

3 Remove the chicken from the pot, peel off and discard the skin and cut into joints. Strain the stock into a bowl; it is brilliant as a soup base and can be frozen for later use if preferred.

Why free range is best for both palate and poultry

Although a free-range chicken is more expensive than a typical supermarket bird, it will more than make up for its price in both flavor and the quality of broth its bones produce. As these birds are older, their carcasses are more developed, so the stock they make contains more protein—and savory deliciousness—while you can feel sure the chickens' lives have been happier, too.

Roasted guinea fowl with lemon & garlic

This is a very easy, rustic dish and is delicious served with minted peas. Guinea fowl is a lean meat with a lot of flavor and makes a great alternative to chicken. It's not gamey enough to upset sensitive palates, and it has an interesting taste that makes it a popular dish. Look for it at specialty meat or Asian markets.

Serves 4
Preparation time 15 minutes
Cooking time 45 minutes

3lb guinea fowl
olive oil, for the dish, plus extra
    to drizzle if necessary
sea salt and black pepper
1 garlic head, broken into cloves,
    skin left on
4 thyme sprigs
2 rosemary sprigs
1 lemon, cut into wedges
2 carrots, roughly chopped
¾lb new potatoes
1 red onion, cut into wedges

1 Preheat the oven to 400°F. Joint the guinea fowl (*see* secret, below).

2 Lightly oil a deep ovenproof dish and add the guinea fowl. Sprinkle with salt and pepper and roll the joints to coat. Add the garlic, herb sprigs, and lemon wedges. Cook in the oven for 20–25 minutes.

3 Meanwhile, bring a pan of water to a boil over high heat, add the carrots and potatoes and boil for 5–10 minutes, until half cooked. Drain and set aside.

4 Remove the guinea fowl from the oven, tip the carrots, potatoes, and onion into the dish and drizzle over a little more oil if the bird seems dry. Return to the oven for 10–15 minutes. Check the guinea fowl is cooked by piercing through the thickest part of a thigh to the bone with a skewer; the juices should run clear. Remove the garlic, herb sprigs, and lemon wedges before serving.

Cutting up whole birds
Arm yourself with sturdy kitchen scissors or, even better, poultry shears. Turn the bird on its breast and remove the backbone. Feel where the thighs attach to the body, cut through, then separate the drumsticks from the thighs. Chop either side of the breastbone to remove both breasts and wings, then halve each so that one piece has the wing attached. Snip off the wing tips. Trim all the pieces and reserve the bones and trimmings for stock.

Quick & easy meat

Indian lamb chops · Homemade lamb sausages in prosciutto

Lamb kidneys in cream & mushroom sauce · Pork loin with pancetta & sage

Pork chops with honey & mustard glaze · simple pork stir-fry

Breaded veal scallops with mozzarella & tomato & red pepper sauce

sirloin steak flavoured with anchovy & garlic · spicy chicken wings

Marinated duck breasts · Chinese duck breast wraps

Turkey scallops with mashed butternut squash & corn

Turkey masala kebabs

Secrets of quick &
easy meat

Meats that are quick to cook tend to be more expensive than others. Tender cuts, such as steak and chops, need just a blast of heat to sear and you pay for the fact that the meat isn't sinewy and tough. But with some recipes you can't skimp. The way to make it work for your family budget is to buy the main ingredient—the duck breast or pork loin—first, then plan around it with cheap, seasonal vegetables. I love steak, salad, and French fries—it's my favorite meal in the world—but it's always a treat. And there's never even a tiny bit wasted.

But many quick-cook meats won't harm your wallet. My Spicy Chicken Wings (*see* page 62) are economical and popular with everyone.

Another inexpensive way to approach quick meat is to use offal. It's easy to feel squeamish about this, but my Lamb Kidneys in Cream & Mushroom Sauce (*see* page 50) are delicious and full of iron and essential nutrients. Previous generations were well aware of the health benefits of eating offal and, though I'm not a massive fan, I do eat it because it's good for me and my family.

Everyone should know how to prepare a stir-fry (*see* page 56). It's a healthy, quick, and easy dish that's great for using up leftovers. There are no rules about what you can and can't include. The only thing to remember is not to leave it in the pan for too long: you want fresh, crunchy vegetables.

Kebabs are a wonderful secret weapon to have in your repertoire and you should try my Turkey Masala Kebabs (*see* page 67). Children love them, especially if they've helped to thread the skewers, and they're fun to eat.

Lamb chops are among the most versatile and speedy of main-course meats and we eat them a lot in our house. They take wonderfully to all sorts of strong seasonings, such as those in my recipe for Indian Lamb Chops (*see* page 46), and they also go well with tomato, rosemary, and garlic.

You can't just leave these dishes to cook, as you can some of the recipes in the Slow & Easy Meat chapter (*see* pages 12–41), and they need more monitoring than oven-baked dishes. So I often cook these quicker dishes for Gordon and myself later in the evenings when my hands are free from children.

Indian lamb chops

This wonderfully warming dish is delicious with my Healthy Couscous (see page 118) and with the broccoli and almond accompaniment on page 54. And, of course, it's great to have a lot of recipes for chops in your culinary arsenal!

Serves 2
Preparation time 10 minutes,
    plus 30 minutes–1 hour marinating
Cooking time 20 minutes
Can be made in advance to end of step 1

½ cup plain yogurt
1 garlic clove, crushed
2 tbsp ground coriander
1 tsp ground turmeric
1 tbsp coriander seeds, crushed
1 tsp paprika
juice of 1 lime (about 2 tbsp)
1½ tbsp cilantro leaves
sea salt and black pepper
4 loin lamb chops (each about 5½oz)
Healthy Couscous, My Style
    (*see* page 118), to serve

1 Place the yogurt, garlic, coriander, turmeric, coriander seeds, paprika, lime juice, cilantro, salt, and pepper into a large bowl and mix together well. Add the lamb chops and toss them in this marinade, to coat well. Cover the bowl with plastic wrap and leave to marinate in the refrigerator for between 30 minutes and 1 hour.

2 Preheat the oven to 400°F.

3 Remove the chops from the marinade and place them into an ovenproof dish (discard the marinade). Cook in the oven for about 20 minutes for meat that is a little pink in the center—perfect for me—or leave them for 5–10 minutes longer if you prefer well-done meat.

4 Serve hot accompanied by my Healthy Couscous.

Why use a yogurt marinade?

Yogurt is an invaluable secret weapon in a meat marinade, as the peoples of Southeast and eastern Asia have always known. Its cultures and mild acidity mean it penetrates right through the meat and acts as a tenderizer, breaking down the tough fibers to prepare the pieces for cooking. The longer you can leave meat in a yogurt marinade, the more tender it becomes.

Homemade lamb sausages in prosciutto

You don't need any fancy equipment or ingredients to make your own sausages. I wrap ground lamb in slices of delicious prosciutto for my moist, spicy bangers. Try making these in a smaller, slimmer size and serving as a canapé, with a minted cucumber and yogurt dip.

Serves 4 (makes 12 sausages)
Preparation time 15–20 minutes
Cooking time 20–25 minutes
Can be made in advance to end of step 3

1lb 2oz ground lamb
1 tbsp ground coriander
2 tbsp ground cumin
½ red onion, finely chopped
3 tbsp chopped parsley
1 chile, seeded and finely chopped
4 tbsp bread crumbs
1 egg, beaten
sea salt and black pepper
12 slices prosciutto
olive oil, for the baking sheet

1 Preheat the oven to 375°F.

2 Place the lamb in a large mixing bowl and break up a little with a fork. Add the coriander, cumin, onion, parsley, chile, and bread crumbs. Mix thoroughly, then add the egg. Season very well with salt and pepper.

3 Divide the mixture into 12 equal-size balls. With wet hands, roll these into sausages (*see* secret, page 24). Tightly wrap each sausage in a slice of prosciutto, leaving both ends open.

4 Place the sausages on a lightly oiled baking sheet, and bake for 20–25 minutes, or until golden brown and cooked through.

The best ground meat

Once ground meat oxidizes it turns dull brown, so avoid buying any that doesn't have a healthy reddish tone as this shows its age. I always try to buy meat ground from lean cuts. If you grind the meat yourself (though I never do!) you'll know exactly what's in it, including how much fat. Many food processors come with a grinding attachment (you'll find it at the bottom of your dustiest kitchen cupboard), or you can simply chop the meat in the food processor.

Lamb kidneys in cream & mushroom sauce

When I was a child, my mother used to serve this to us on toast. It's a great way to encourage children to eat kidneys. My mother was way ahead of her time, as these days offal of all sorts is the height of culinary fashion in the best restaurants.

Serves 2
Preparation time 10 minutes
Cooking time 15 minutes

9¾oz lamb kidneys, trimmed
   (*see* secret, below)
sea salt and black pepper
2 tbsp all-purpose flour, to dust
1 tbsp olive oil
2 tbsp unsalted butter
2 shallots, finely chopped
3½oz mushrooms, roughly chopped
1 cup plus 2 tbsp dry white wine
1 cup plus 2 tbsp chicken stock
⅓ cup heavy cream
1 heaping tsp grainy mustard
2 tbsp chopped flatleaf parsley
2 thick slices whole wheat bread

1 Cut the kidneys into ¾in chunks and season generously with salt and pepper. Sprinkle over the flour and toss to coat evenly. Pour the oil into a skillet and place over high heat until smoking. Add the kidneys to the pan, being careful to avoid splashes. Keep a close eye on them, turning so they color all over but don't burn, then remove them to a bowl. They should be seared but not cooked through.

2 Place the butter in the pan over medium heat and, when it has melted, add the shallots. Sauté for 2–3 minutes, or until softened. Add the mushrooms and continue to cook for 3 minutes.

3 Pour in the white wine and boil until the liquid has reduced by two-thirds. Pour in the stock and allow it to reduce by half, then add the cream and any juices from the bowl of kidneys. Allow the sauce to bubble gently and thicken, then add the mustard. Reduce the heat now so the contents of the pan are no longer bubbling or the mixture will separate.

4 Return the kidneys to the pan and stir to coat in the sauce and cook through. Add the parsley and cook, stirring, for 5 minutes. Meanwhile, toast the bread. Serve the kidneys on the toast with sauce.

How to trim kidneys

Of course, you can get your butcher to trim kidneys, but sometimes—and especially if you shop at farmers' markets—you will have to buy them whole. Don't be discouraged! Simply peel off the membrane covering the kidneys, then, with a pair of scissors, cut them in half and trim out the tough white core from each piece. Never overcook kidneys or they go rubbery; make sure they remain succulently pink within.

Pork loin with pancetta & sage

This dish looks very fancy, wrapped in its pancetta jacket, but it's beautifully simple to make. Accompanied by polenta and a dressed arugula salad, it is smart enough to serve at any supper party. Or have it as a romantic meal for two; any leftovers are delicious cold.

Serves 4
Preparation time 10 minutes
Cooking time 30 minutes
Can be made in advance to end of step 3
Suitable for freezing

12 pancetta strips, or bacon
sea salt and black pepper
12 small sage leaves
11½oz pork tenderloin
1 tbsp olive oil

1 Preheat the oven to 350°F.

2 Cover the surface of your chopping board with a layer of plastic wrap, then lay out the pancetta strips, slightly overlapping each other. Season well with pepper, then put a sage leaf on each strip. Place the pork on top, at a right angle to the pancetta strips, season with salt and pepper, then lift up the plastic wrap to roll the loin in pancetta. Remove the plastic wrap.

3 Tear a piece of aluminum foil big enough to wrap the loin and season the foil with salt and pepper. Place the pork on the foil, then turn it through the seasoning. Tightly roll up the foil around the meat, twisting each end to seal. Cut off any excess foil.

4 Place the foil parcel in the oven for 15 minutes, then remove and leave until cool enough to handle. Turn the oven up to 400°F.

5 Remove the foil, place the loin on a baking sheet and sprinkle with oil. Return it to the oven for 10 minutes, or until the loin is cooked and the pancetta is crisp.

Making pork loin juicy

Pork tenderloin is a relatively expensive cut, as it is very lean. However, being lean also makes it prone to drying out and turning to dust in the mouth unless treated with care. Wrapping the loin in pancetta, as in this recipe, will solve the problem and result in succulent, juicy meat. Bacon does the same job, if you can't find pancetta.

Pork chops with honey & mustard glaze

This recipe features steamed vegetables. Steaming is a really healthy way of cooking as you don't lose the nutrients or flavor that you do when boiling vegetables. The honey and mustard glaze would be equally good spread over baby back ribs, which are popular with my children.

Serves 4
Preparation time 5 minutes
Cooking time 30 minutes

4 pork chops (each about 6oz)
sea salt and black pepper
1 tbsp olive oil
1 cup purple-sprouting broccoli or
    broccolini, trimmed
1 tbsp chili oil
1 garlic clove, finely chopped
1 chile, seeded and finely chopped
3 tbsp sliced almonds

For the honey & mustard glaze
3 tbsp Dijon mustard
2 tbsp golden honey
2 tsp soy sauce

1 Preheat the oven to 375°F.

2 For the honey and mustard glaze, mix together all the ingredients with a pinch of salt in a small bowl.

3 Season both sides of the pork chops with salt and pepper. Pour the olive oil into a large skillet over high heat, add the chops and cook for 2–3 minutes on each side, until lightly golden brown. Lay the chops on a baking sheet and spread on the honey and mustard topping, then bake for 25 minutes. To ensure they are cooked through, remove a chop from the oven and slice it through with a sharp knife. If any trace of pink remains inside, return to the oven for 2–3 minutes more, then test again.

4 Meanwhile, in a steamer or microwave, cook the broccoli for 4–5 minutes, or until tender. Heat the chili oil in a skillet or wok over medium heat, then toss in the garlic, chile, and almonds and cook for 3–4 minutes, stirring, until toasted. Add the broccoli and stir to coat in the garlic, chile, and almonds. Serve immediately alongside the chops.

Preparing a pork chop
Using a sharp pair of scissors or sharp knife, snip through the rind and fat at 1in intervals along the length of each chop. This will prevent it from curling up during cooking.

Simple pork stir-fry

You can use whatever vegetables you like in this recipe; it's a handy way to finish up any odds and ends that you may have knocking about in the refrigerator.

Serves 4
Preparation time 15 minutes
Cooking time 10 minutes

2 tbsp all-purpose flour
sea salt and black pepper
1 pork tenderloin (about 1lb 5oz),
    thinly sliced
2 tbsp olive oil
3 carrots, cut into thin sticks
1 red bell pepper, seeded and thinly sliced
1 green bell pepper, seeded and
    thinly sliced
24 green beans, trimmed
20 small button mushrooms
juice of 1 lemon (about 3 tbsp)
generous splash of soy sauce
3 tsp Thai fish sauce
1lb 2oz fresh egg noodles

1 Put the flour into a resealable plastic bag, season very well, and shake gently to mix. Add the pork, seal the bag, and shake well to coat. Pour into a fine-mesh strainer to remove any excess flour. Meanwhile, bring a large pan of salted water to a boil.

2 Pour the oil into a large skillet or wok over high heat. Drop in the pork and stir for 1–2 minutes, until all sides are brown. Add the vegetables and toss, then pour in the lemon juice, soy sauce, and fish sauce, and stir-fry for 5–10 minutes, until the vegetables are tender but still crisp and the pork is cooked through. To test the pork, remove a piece to a plate and slice it. There should be no trace of pink. If there is, continue to stir-fry for 1 minute, then test again.

3 Meanwhile, cook the noodles in boiling water as directed on the package, then drain. Divide the noodles between 4 warmed plates and serve the pork and vegetables on the top.

How to make a stir-fry
Stir-frying is quick-cooking over high heat using very little oil, while constantly moving the food around the pan. The most time-consuming part is preparing the ingredients: cut all vegetables to roughly the same size so they cook evenly. The exception to this is if you are using greens, such as bok choi, which should be added just 3–4 minutes before the end of the cooking time so that they remain tender yet crisp rather than overcooked and soggy. Prepare all the vegetables in advance as there will be no spare time during cooking. If the pan seems dry during stir-frying, add a splash of water to help steam the vegetables and amalgamate all the flavorings.

Breaded veal scallops with mozzarella & tomato & red pepper sauce

I was appearing on "Hell's Kitchen" in the States as a contestant, in disguise so Gordon wouldn't recognize me. This is what I cooked: it's a favorite recipe of mine. If you can find the super-buttery burrata cheese, use it instead of mozzarella, though this is delicious either way.

Serves 2
Preparation time 40–45 minutes
Cooking time 30 minutes
Can be made in advance to end of step 4
**Suitable for freezing (meat and sauce
   separately) at end of step 4**

2 veal cutlets (each about 7oz)
2½ cups bread crumbs
1 tbsp dried oregano
¼ cup finely grated Parmesan cheese
sea salt and black pepper
1 egg, beaten
2 tbsp all-purpose flour
2 tbsp olive oil
juice of ¼ lemon (about 2 tsp)
9oz buffalo mozzarella cheese
3 basil leaves, shredded

For the sauce
1 tbsp olive oil
3 shallots, finely chopped
2 garlic cloves, finely chopped
2 red chiles, seeded and finely chopped
1½ cups cherry tomatoes, halved
1 small yellow bell pepper, seeded and
   thinly sliced
handful of basil leaves, finely chopped
2 tbsp Worcestershire sauce
splash of sherry vinegar

1 To make the sauce, pour the oil into a large skillet over medium heat, add the shallots, garlic, and chiles, and sauté for 2–3 minutes until softened but not colored. Add the tomatoes, yellow pepper, basil, and Worcestershire sauce. Season with salt and pepper and cook gently for 15–20 minutes. Toward the end of cooking time, stir in the vinegar.

2 Remove the sauce from the heat, pour into a blender and process until smooth. You may have to do this in batches as the blender should be no more than half full each time to avoid splashing; hold the lid on with a clean kitchen towel to protect your hands from the hot liquid. Set aside.

3 Flatten each piece of veal until ½in thick (*see* secret, page 66).

4 Mix together the bread crumbs, oregano, and Parmesan and season with salt and pepper. Spread this coating on a plate. Pour the egg onto a second plate and place the flour on a third. Season the flour very well with salt and pepper and mix to combine. Place the three plates side by side. Coat the veal scallops in the flour, shake off any excess, then turn through the egg, ensuring all surfaces are covered. Finally, press the veal into the bread crumbs, coating both sides. If you have time, put the scallops on a plate, cover, and refrigerate for 30 minutes to help the coating to stick. Return to room temperature before continuing.

For the arugula salad
handful of arugula leaves
1 tbsp olive oil
½ tbsp aged balsamic vinegar

To serve
handful of Parmesan cheese shavings
2 lemon wedges

5 Place a large skillet over medium-high heat, pour in the oil and, when it is hot, add the veal and brown lightly on both sides. Reduce the heat and cook slowly for 4–5 minutes. Squeeze the lemon juice over the meat just before the end of cooking. Remove the scallops from the pan and place on paper towels to blot off any excess oil.

6 Heat the broiler to its highest setting. Pour the pureed sauce into a saucepan and gently reheat. Put the veal onto the broiler pan. Slice the mozzarella into 6 slices and lay 3 slices on each scallop. Place under the hot broiler and allow the cheese to melt, then sprinkle the basil on top.

7 Meanwhile, place the arugula into a small bowl and pour in the oil and vinegar. Turn lightly with your hands to coat.

8 Put each scallop on a warmed plate, spoon over the sauce and sprinkle with Parmesan shavings. Add a lemon wedge and serve with the dressed arugula salad.

Choosing happy veal

Buy natural, pastured veal, which is ethically produced and has a pink color. This way you can feel satisfied that the calves have been kept and slaughtered humanely. Avoid milk-fed veal, which produces a much paler meat: the standards of welfare for these animals are very poor.

Sirloin steak flavoured with anchovy & garlic

The flavors here complement one another beautifully; this is a wonderfully different way of cooking great steak. It's so good I'd eat it twice a week if I could! The steak I used was more or less 1in thick, and the timings here will produce a medium-rare steak. This is fantastic served with a crisp, green salad or broiled vine tomatoes.

Serves 1
Preparation time 5 minutes,
   plus 1–2 hours marinating
Cooking time 5 minutes

10oz sirloin steak
3 canned anchovy fillets in olive oil
2 garlic cloves, very finely sliced

1 Using a small, sharp knife, make about 10 slits all the way through the steak.

2 Drain the anchovies, reserving their oil, and slice into 1in pieces. Press a piece of anchovy and a slice of garlic into each slit on the steak. Pour the anchovy oil over the top of the steak and rub it in. Cover with plastic wrap and leave to marinate in the refrigerator for 1–2 hours, removing 30 minutes before cooking as the meat should be cooked from room temperature.

3 Heat a nonstick skillet over high heat. When it is smoking, lay in the steak. Allow it to brown nicely on the underside for about 2 minutes. Turn it over and cook for another 2–3 minutes (*see* secret, left, for tips on knowing when your steak is done to your liking). Tip the pan so the fat crisps and browns as well.

4 Place the steak on a warmed plate and allow to rest for 5 minutes before serving.

The perfect steak

Start with your meat at room temperature and make sure your pan is red-hot; if it's too cool, the steak will be tough. Turn the steak only once during cooking. It's impossible to generalize about how long to cook it, as that depends on the size, cut, and thickness of your meat. Instead, poke it! A rare steak will feel soft; well-done will feel firm; medium will be somewhere in between the two. Rest the steak for 5 minutes before serving.

Spicy chicken wings

This recipe's harshest critic is my 9-year-old son. A favorite local restaurant of his apparently does "the best," mine are second best... But this is a marvelous recipe and easy to have on the table in an instant. Supply lots of paper towels for the inevitable mess!

Serves 4
Preparation time 5–10 minutes,
   plus 2–24 hours marinating
Cooking time 20–25 minutes
Can be made in advance to end of step 1
Suitable for freezing at end of step 1

6 tbsp hoisin sauce
2 tbsp sesame oil
4 tbsp golden honey
3 tbsp hot chili sauce
2 tbsp dark soy sauce
2 tbsp grainy mustard
24 chicken wings

1 Place all the ingredients except the chicken in a large bowl and mix thoroughly, then pour into a large resealable plastic bag. Add the chicken wings, seal the bag, and turn the wings, massaging to make sure they are completely covered with a generous amount of marinade (*see* secret, below left). Ensure the bag is well sealed, put it into a large bowl, and place in the refrigerator to marinate for between 2 and 24 hours.

2 Remove the chicken from the refrigerator and bring to room temperature. Meanwhile, preheat the oven to 425°F.

3 Space out the wings on a baking sheet lined with parchment paper. Cook in the oven, turning once, for 20–25 minutes, until deliciously crispy and sticky. To test they're done, pierce a wing through the thickest part right to the bone with a small, sharp knife. The juices should run clear; if there is any trace of pink, return to the oven for a couple of minutes, then test again.

4 Watch your fingers, as the wings will be very hot and you won't resist them for long!

Marinating meat

I use a resealable plastic bag for marinating meat, as it causes less mess than other methods. Pour in the marinade, add the meat, seal the bag, and massage through the bag so the meat is evenly coated. Make sure the bag is completely sealed before refrigerating; putting the bag in a bowl will also minimize the risk of leakage. If you would rather marinate directly in a bowl, always use non-reactive plastic or glass, as metals may react to ingredients in a marinade, and cover the bowl. The longer you leave the meat to marinate, the more it will tenderize and the more intense the flavor will be. Poultry can be left in the refrigerator for 2–24 hours and red meat can usually be marinated overnight. Never re-use marinade, as there is a risk of food poisoning.

Marinated duck breasts

These are lovely for a romantic meal. Unlike chicken, duck can be served rare and juicy if you like. The cooking time I give here will produce beautifully juicy, medium duck breasts. If you prefer yours well done, continue to cook them for a few minutes more on each side.

Serves 2
Preparation time 5–10 minutes,
    plus 30 minutes–24 hours marinating
Cooking time 15 minutes

2 skinless duck breasts (each about 5oz)
splash of olive oil

For the marinade
1in fresh ginger, peeled and
    sliced lengthwise
2 garlic cloves, halved lengthwise
6 tbsp soy sauce
2 tbsp toasted sesame oil
1 tbsp golden honey

1 Mix together all the marinade ingredients and pour into a shallow dish. Lay the duck breasts into the marinade and turn to coat, then cover with plastic wrap and leave to marinate at room temperature for 30 minutes, or in the refrigerator for up to 24 hours.

2 Remove the duck from the marinade; reserve the liquid. Put the oil in a nonstick skillet over medium-high heat. Once it is hot, add the duck and cook for 2–3 minutes on each side, until caramelized (make sure the heat is not too high or the honey will burn). Add the marinade and allow it to bubble and thicken. Continue to cook for 5–10 minutes, turning occasionally. This will produce a medium-rare duck breast. If the marinade is too syrupy, add a splash of hot water to dilute.

3 Remove the duck from the heat and allow to rest for 5 minutes, then slice. Serve with the sauce spooned over.

Preparing duck breasts

I use skinless duck for this recipe, but often you'll want to serve it with skin and fat intact. With a sharp knife, trim off excess fat. Score the skin (but don't penetrate the flesh unless you are going to marinate the duck before cooking) to allow the fat to run out. Season and place skin-side down into a hot, dry, nonstick skillet. Cook until the skin is crisp, then turn to cook the other side.

Chinese duck breast wraps

I used to make this with Chinese pancakes, which are delicious but can be hard to find. So now I use lettuce, which results in a lighter, healthier dish. To make this as a canapé, use baby Little Gem (baby Romaine) leaves as a "cup" for the duck and slice the breast widthwise.

Serves 4
Preparation time 20 minutes, plus
  30 minutes or overnight marinating
Cooking time 25 minutes
Sauce can be made in advance (*see* step 4)

pinch of salt
4 tbsp golden honey
3 tbsp soy sauce
1 tsp ground star anise
4 duck breasts (each about 4½oz), skin on
½ cucumber, seeded and cut into matchsticks
8 scallions, cut into matchsticks
12 large Iceberg lettuce leaves

For the sauce
14.5oz can chopped tomatoes
4 tbsp hoisin sauce
few drops of chili sauce
4 garlic cloves, crushed
4 tbsp soy sauce
2 tbsp rice wine vinegar
2 tsp ground coriander
1 tsp cinnamon
½ tsp Chinese five spice

1 Mix together the salt, honey, soy sauce, and star anise and pour into a shallow dish.

2 Lay the duck breasts on a board, skin-side up. Make slits widthwise across each breast about ½in apart, deep enough to cut through the skin and fat and penetrate the flesh. Place the duck into the marinade and turn to coat, then cover with plastic wrap and place in the refrigerator for at least 30 minutes or overnight. The flavor will improve the longer you leave them.

3 Preheat the oven to 375°F.

4 Place all the ingredients for the sauce into a pan, set over medium heat until it bubbles, then reduce the heat and leave to simmer for 10 minutes. Allow to cool, pour into a bowl, cover and set aside. The sauce will keep for up to 10 days in the refrigerator, but make sure it comes to room temperature before you use it.

5 Place a nonstick skillet over high heat. Add the duck breasts, skin-side down, and allow them to sear and render their fat for about 4 minutes. Turn and cook the flesh side for another 4 minutes, then place the duck on a baking sheet and cook in the oven for 15 minutes. Remove and allow to rest for 10 minutes (*see* secret, left).

6 Slice each duck breast lengthwise, as thinly as you can, into long strips. Serve each sliced breast on the side of a warmed plate and provide the sauce, cucumber, scallions and lettuce on the table, allowing guests to roll their own wraps.

Meat and heat
Never take meat straight from the refrigerator, cook and serve it instantly— the outside will overcook before the center heats up. Take it out of the refrigerator at least 20 minutes before cooking (up to 1 hour for larger roasts). After cooking, rest meat for at least 10 minutes; it becomes far more succulent. Large roasts will need 20–30 minutes, insulated with foil.

Turkey scallops with mashed butternut squash & corn

Turkey is very lean, and it's not very expensive. It is wonderful for all those people who only really enjoy eating white meat, as it has tons of flavor. Pick some up next time you're at the supermarket—don't save it for the holidays.

Serves 4
Preparation time 15 minutes
Cooking time 30 minutes

drizzle of olive oil, preferably lemon-infused
8 turkey cutlets (each about 6oz), pounded
    into ½in thick scallops (*see* secret, below)
2 ears of sweet corn
2 tsp butter

For the squash
2 tbsp olive oil
1 butternut squash (about 2lb 4oz),
    peeled and diced
2 rosemary sprigs
1 garlic clove, finely chopped
knob of butter (about 2 tbsp)
sea salt and black pepper
2 tbsp crème fraîche
splash of milk

1 Preheat the oven to 375°F.

2 Begin with the squash. Drizzle the oil in a roasting pan, add the squash, rosemary, garlic, and butter. Season with salt and pepper. Roast for 25 minutes, or until the squash is tender.

3 Meanwhile, bring a large saucepan of salted water to a boil over high heat. Cut each ear of corn in half and insert wooden skewers into both ends of each piece. Add the corn to the boiling water and cook for 8 minutes, or until tender.

4 Pour the oil for the scallops into a skillet and place over high heat until hot. Season both sides of the turkey pieces and fry for just 2 minutes each side. Check they are cooked by removing a scallop to a plate and slicing it through; if any trace of pink remains inside, place in the pan for 30 seconds more, then test again.

5 Remove the squash from the oven and discard the rosemary. Transfer the squash to a large mixing bowl and add the crème fraîche and milk. Mash until smooth, then taste and adjust the seasoning. Cover with foil and keep warm in a low oven.

6 Serve the turkey on warmed plates with a spoonful of squash and a piece of corn, each with a little butter melting over the top.

Pounding out scallops

Place the meat pieces between 2 sheets of plastic wrap on a work surface. Gently pound with a rolling pin or meat mallet until they are about ½in thick. The plastic wrap will prevent the meat from tearing, protect your work surface and keep the process hygienic.

Turkey masala kebabs

A lot of people overcook turkey, and therefore have the mistaken impression that it's a dry meat. It isn't; it's juicy and has a great depth of flavor. Just pay attention and cook it as carefully as you would any other lean meat. You will need 8 skewers for these kebabs.

Serves 4 (makes 8)
Preparation time 10 minutes,
   plus 15 minutes or overnight marinating
Cooking time 20 minutes
Can be made in advance to end of step 3

1lb 7oz turkey breast, diced
3 tbsp masala curry paste
16 large button mushrooms, stems removed
1 red bell pepper, seeded and cut into
   1in dice
1 yellow bell pepper, seeded and cut into
   1in dice
1 red onion, cut into 1in chunks
1 large zucchini, cut into 1in rounds
3 tbsp olive oil

1 Preheat the oven to 400°F.

2 Place the turkey in a mixing bowl, spoon in the curry paste, and stir to coat. Cover with plastic wrap and leave to marinate for 15 minutes at room temperature, or overnight in the refrigerator if you are organized enough!

3 Arrange all the vegetables in bowls. Thread a mushroom onto each skewer, then alternate the turkey and other vegetables. Finish off with another mushroom.

4 Put the kebabs on a baking sheet, place in the oven and cook for 10 minutes, then turn over and cook for 10 minutes more, or until the turkey is cooked through. Check a piece of meat by slicing it through; if any trace of pink remains inside, return to the oven for a minute more, then test again.

5 Serve the kebabs on warmed plates, allowing 2 skewers per person.

Talking diced turkey
Readily available, lean, and relatively inexpensive, turkey should not be saved only for Thanksgiving! Most diced turkey you can buy is breast meat, which has a tendency to be dry because it contains almost no fat. Although the meat must always be fully cooked through for safety—as is the case with chicken—you should take care to avoid overcooking as dry turkey has an unpleasant, dusty texture.

Fish

Moroccan fish tagine · Salmon fillet in black sauce · Spanish fish soup

Pollack & shrimp pie with smoked paprika mashed potato topping

Salt-baked dorade · Broiled tuna & vegetable kebabs

Seared coriander-crusted tuna steaks with miso

Smoked haddock fish cakes · Thai red curry · Crab & sweet corn soup

Sautéed calamari with chorizo & peppers · Mussels with Belgian beer

Secrets of cooking fish

With fish and shellfish, timings are vital as you must never overcook them. Poaching is a really good way to start off if you're new to fish cookery. You'll know the fish is ready when you can gently flake the flesh with a fork.

It's impressive to cook a whole fish. I learned how to salt-bake fish (*see* page 82) when I was hosting a TV cooking show and it is among the most eye-popping dishes to bring to the table when you have friends for dinner.

Try cooking fillets of fish *en papillote*: place them on a large square of parchment paper, then add the seasonings you like, such as lemon or herbs, and a knob of butter. Seal the parchment paper into a parcel around the fish and bake until you can gently flake the flesh. When you open the package at the table, you will get a fantastic waft of fragrances.

People get scared of shellfish but, if you follow my simple tips—for instance, in my Mussels with Belgian Beer (*see* page 98)—you will quickly learn that it's easy to cook them safely. And they are super-speedy: you don't have to do a lot with them.

With careful shopping, ready-cooked fish can make an instant appetizer. Buy shrimp for a cocktail and serve with my Tomato & Tarragon Mayonnaise (*see* page 272) for a new twist on an old favorite. Dressed crab is always impressive. Or, if you're feeling flush, try a lobster roll with arugula and mayonnaise for a treat that takes hardly any time at all.

Though fish needs exact timings, don't be put off. The base for my Thai Red Curry (*see* page 92) can be made the day before; in fact it improves with reheating, so makes a quick and easy supper.

It's good to know how to make a comforting fish pie (*see* page 78). You can use a sustainable fish such as Alaskan pollack, and hide a multitude of vegetables from the children in the sauce! My recipe has a delicious paprika topping, but it's also nice topped with puff pastry. After a recent half-marathon I had three helpings.

Fish is wonderfully good for you. We have it once or twice a week and always make a point of eating oily fish such as salmon. I stick to the rule of fish on a Friday, which was the way it was at my school.

Moroccan fish tagine

I make this simple tagine for the children, taking care not to add too much salt. The lemon compensates for the lack of salt and works well with the peppers and tomatoes. When cooking this for adults, I fry two merguez sausages, cut them into chunks, along with the peppers, and sprinkle in 2 tablespoons rinsed capers before baking.

Serves 6
Preparation time 10 minutes,
    plus 30 minutes marinating
Cooking time 35 minutes
Can be made in advance to end of step 4

3 garlic cloves, crushed
2 tsp ground cumin
3 tsp paprika
3 tbsp tomato puree
6 tbsp lemon juice
6 monkfish fillets (5½oz each), skinned
1 tbsp olive oil
2 red bell peppers, seeded and cut into
    ¾in dice
15 cherry tomatoes, sliced
sea salt and black pepper
small handful of cilantro leaves, chopped

Adding flavor to fish

Marinating fish is easy. Simply mix your chosen acid ingredients (such as lemon juice or vinegar) with oils (such as extra-virgin olive oil), seasonings, and herbs and pour them over the fish in a nonreactive glass or plastic bowl before refrigerating for 20–30 minutes. Be careful not to leave it any longer or the acids will start to "cook" the fish, producing a mushy texture.

1 In a nonreactive glass or plastic bowl, mix together the garlic, cumin, paprika, tomato puree, and lemon juice. Put the monkfish into the bowl, rub it all over with the spice mixture, then cover the bowl with plastic wrap. Leave to marinate in the refrigerator for 30 minutes.

2 Preheat the oven to 375°F.

3 Heat a nonstick skillet over medium heat, pour in the oil, add the peppers and cook, stirring, for 2–3 minutes until softened.

4 Lay half the tomatoes and cooked peppers in an ovenproof dish and arrange the monkfish fillets on top. Scatter with the remaining tomatoes and peppers. Season with salt and pepper and cover the dish with foil.

5 Bake for 25–30 minutes, or until the fish is firm and cooked through. To test, firmly press a fillet with the back of a fork. It should start to break into opaque flakes. If it looks translucent inside, cook for 2–3 minutes more before testing again.

6 Sprinkle the tagine with the cilantro and serve on a bed of basmati rice or mashed butternut squash (*see* page 66).

Salmon fillet in black sauce

This dish is delicious served with peapods and wild rice. The crunchiness of the vegetables and nutty quality of the rice really complement the strong, salty-sweet flavors of the glaze on the moist fish. And this is one of the easiest recipes in the whole book!

Serves 2
Preparation time 5 minutes
Cooking time 15 minutes

4 tbsp soy sauce
2 tbsp sesame oil
2 tbsp golden honey
1lb 2oz skinless salmon fillet,
    cut into 2 pieces

1 Preheat the oven to 350°F.

2 Mix together the soy sauce, sesame oil, and honey in a small bowl. Place the salmon fillets in a shallow baking pan, spoon over the marinade and gently rub it into the top of the fish. Cook in the oven for 10–15 minutes, removing occasionally to spoon the sauce back over the salmon.

3 Remove from the oven and allow to rest for 5 minutes, then serve drizzled with any of the marinade that remains on the baking pan.

How to skin a piece of fish
If you buy salmon with the skin on, don't panic! It's easy to remove. Place the salmon skin-side down on a board. Take hold of one corner and insert a fine-tipped knife blade—ideally a filleting knife as the blade is flexible—between skin and flesh. Firmly grab the corner of the skin and, using a zig-zag motion, slice the skin away from the flesh, keeping the knife as close to the skin as you can.

Spanish fish soup

Any flaky white fish would be excellent in this soup; I have chosen whiting (also called silver hake, or hake) as it is inexpensive. Ask your fishmonger what's best, and of course be guided by what is the best value and sustainable; the two usually go hand in hand.

Serves 4
Preparation time 15 minutes
Cooking time 25 minutes

2¼oz chorizo sausage, roughly chopped
2 tbsp olive oil
1 Spanish onion, roughly chopped
3 garlic cloves, left whole
1 red bell pepper, seeded and finely sliced
1lb 2oz whiting (silver hake), or cod,
    or other flaky white fish, skinned and
    chopped into chunks
¾lb ripe tomatoes, roughly chopped
2¼ cups chicken stock (*see* secret, page 37),
    plus extra to adjust consistency
1 tsp smoked paprika
sea salt and black pepper

1 Place a dry skillet over medium heat, tip in the chorizo and fry until it releases its oil and begins to turn crispy. Set aside.

2 Heat the olive oil in a large pan over medium heat. Tip in the onion and garlic cloves and fry for 6–8 minutes until the onion is soft.

3 Add the red pepper to the onion and gently fry until it softens, too. Add the fish, tomatoes, stock, and smoked paprika and leave these to cook for 15 minutes. Season with salt and pepper to taste.

4 Ladle the soup into a blender and process until smooth. You may have to do this in batches as the blender should be no more than half full each time to prevent splashing; hold the lid on with a kitchen towel to protect your hands from splashes.

5 Return the soup to a clean pan and place over gentle heat to reheat before serving, adding enough extra stock or water to bring it to the consistency you like. Pour the soup into warmed bowls, sprinkle the crispy chorizo on top, then drizzle the surface of each portion with the chorizo oil.

Pork and fish: perfect partners
Although it's not common in Britain beyond the Welsh dish of cockles with bacon, mixing pork with fish is a popular custom among the Spanish and Portuguese. It's an excellent combination, with the succulence of the meat giving an extra dimension to the seafood. Extend the idea and try cold oysters served with hot, spicy sausages, seared scallops with blood sausage, pork with clams, or herrings in cornmeal fried with bacon.

Pollack & shrimp pie with smoked paprika mashed potato topping

A fish pie is like shepherd's pie—with a potato topping rather than a crust. The tomatoes aren't traditional, but they really intensify in flavor as they bake, complementing the dish perfectly along with the smoked paprika and cayenne pepper. Alaskan pollack is sustainable and excellently meaty; ideal for a pie. Use another flaky white fish if pollack is unavailable.

Serves 4–6
Preparation time 20–25 minutes
Cooking time 50 minutes
Can be made in advance

1lb 5oz pollack fillet or other flaky
   white fish, skin on
1lb 2oz raw shrimp, shelled and deveined
2 cups milk
2 bay leaves
6 peppercorns
few parsley stalks
drizzle of olive oil
1 large leek, finely chopped
3½oz pancetta, or bacon, cubed
4 tbsp (½ stick) butter
⅓ cup flour
2 tbsp finely chopped parsley
1 tbsp finely chopped basil

For the topping
3lb 5oz Yukon Gold potatoes,
   cut into even chunks
pinch of salt
knob of butter (about 2 tbsp)
splash of milk
1½ tsp smoked paprika
pinch of cayenne pepper
2 egg yolks
5¾oz cherry tomatoes, halved
2 tsp thyme leaves

1 Begin with the topping. Place the potatoes in a pan of cold water, add the salt and bring to a boil, then reduce the heat and simmer for 15 minutes, until tender. Drain very well (*see* secret, page 20). Add the butter and milk and mash until smooth. Stir in the paprika and cayenne pepper, then stir in the egg yolks. Set aside.

2 Put the pollack and shrimp into a deep pan and add enough of the milk just to cover, then pop in the bay leaves, peppercorns, and parsley stalks. Place over a medium heat until it starts to bubble, then turn off the heat, cover with foil or a lid and leave to cook in the residual heat for 10–15 minutes. Using a slotted spoon, remove the fish and shrimp from the milk. Strain the milk through a strainer into a bowl and set aside. Flake the fish onto a plate, removing the skin and any bones.

3 Heat the oil in a pan and gently fry the leek and pancetta for 2–3 minutes. Remove from the heat and set aside.

4 Preheat the oven to 375°F. Melt the 4 tbsp butter in a saucepan, add the flour and mix to form a thick paste. Whisk in the reserved milk from poaching the fish and shrimp, a little at a time to avoid lumps, until it is all incorporated. Cook for 4–5 minutes, still whisking occasionally, until the sauce is smooth and thick enough to coat the back of a spoon. Stir in the chopped parsley and basil.

Go for sustainable fish

I would like my children to enjoy fish all their lives, as I have, so I always try to buy varieties from stocks that aren't endangered. Pollack is an excellent example of this, and is very underused; its white, meaty, and flaky flesh is perfect for this recipe. If you can't find it, you can use cod instead, but make sure you buy farmed cod so you can tuck in with a clear conscience.

5 Put the pollack and shrimp in an 8-cup ovenproof dish along with the leeks, and pancetta, evenly distributing these ingredients over the bottom of the dish so each serving will have some of everything. Pour in the white sauce and gently stir it through.

6 Spread the potato mixture over the top and smooth with the back of a fork. Arrange the halved tomatoes on top and very gently push them slightly into the potatoes. Sprinkle on the thyme leaves and cook in the oven for 30 minutes, until bubbling and golden.

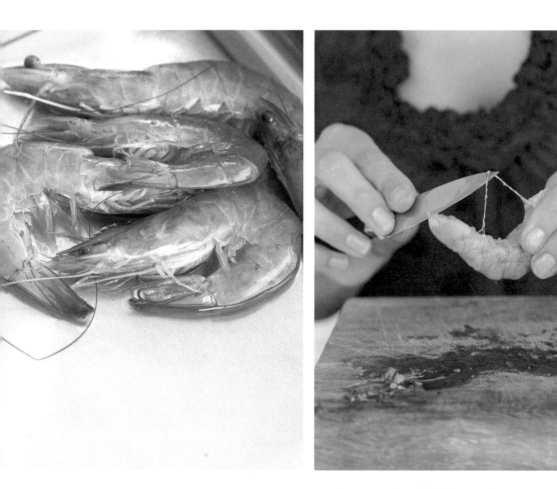

Salt-baked dorade

I had seen fish cooked in this way several times and had always been intrigued, so I came up with this recipe. The fish is steamed in the salt that is packed around it and, when cooked, the flesh is incredibly moist and delicate. Give it a go! This dish is delicious served with steamed broccoli and new potatoes.

Serves 2
Preparation time 10 minutes
Cooking time 25 minutes

3lb 5oz coarse sea salt
3 egg whites
2 whole dorade (1lb each), or other small-medium, deep-bodied white fish, gutted and scaled
1 lemon, sliced
few rosemary or thyme sprigs

1 Preheat the oven to 400°F.

2 Place the sea salt in a large bowl, add the egg whites, and stir them in. Take a large baking pan and pour on a ¾in bed of the salt mixture. Lay the two fish on top so they face top to tail. Insert the lemon slices and herbs into the cavities of each. Close the cavities and pack over a second layer of the salt mixture, again about ¾in thick (*see* secret, below left).

3 Place in the oven for 20–25 minutes until cooked (*see* secret, below left).

4 Remove the top layer of salt and take out the fish. Remove the heads and skin and serve. Alternatively, just place the dish in the middle of the table with a flourish and dig in!

Salt-baking fish
Pick the freshest fish you can find and stuff it with your preferred aromatics: try fennel, orange, or dill. A large fish cooked in this way makes a great centerpiece for the table; take it to the table with the crust cracked and let guests help themselves. You must make sure the fish is entirely encased in the salt mixture as you don't want the fish juices to leak. It is cooked when a firm tap will crack the salty crust.

Broiled tuna & vegetable kebabs

You will need 8 wooden skewers for these kebabs: always pre-soak them in a deep bowl of water for at least 10 minutes before use to prevent burning. Choose sustainable line-caught tuna and serve with fluffy basmati rice, or opt for the lettuce bed recipe here for a lighter option.

Serves 4
Preparation time 10 minutes
Cooking time 20–25 minutes
Can be made in advance to end of step 2

1 red onion, cut into 8 wedges
1 yellow bell pepper, seeded and cut into
   1¼in dice
1 zucchini, cut into 1¼in half-moons
2 tbsp olive oil, plus extra for the vegetables
4 tuna steaks (5oz each), cut into 1in dice
12 cherry tomatoes on the vine
sea salt and black pepper
1 tsp dried parsley
1 tsp dried oregano
juice of 1 lime (about 2 tbsp)

For the lettuce bed (optional)
1 tbsp olive oil
2 heads baby Little Gem lettuces
   (baby Romaine), quartered lengthwise
1 tbsp balsamic vinegar
1 tsp sesame seeds

1 Preheat the oven to 350°F. Put the onion, bell pepper, and zucchini into a roasting dish and drizzle with a little oil. Toss with your hands so that everything is coated. Cook in the oven for 15 minutes, or until softened, then remove.

2 Heat the broiler to its highest setting. Put the tuna into a bowl with the roasted vegetables and the tomatoes. Drizzle with the 2 tbsp oil, season with salt and pepper and add the dried herbs. Toss together to coat with all the seasonings. Thread the ingredients onto the soaked skewers, evenly dividing the pieces of tuna and vegetables between them.

3 Place the kebabs in a broiler pan and slide under the hot broiler for 5–10 minutes, turning frequently. Just before they are ready, squeeze the lime juice over.

4 Meanwhile make the lettuce bed, if you like. Pour the oil into a large skillet placed over high heat, add the lettuce and stir until it very slightly browns at the edges. Add the vinegar and sesame seeds and stir. Serve the kebabs on the lettuce bed.

How to choose and cook tuna

When buying tuna, go for chunky steaks that a bright, rich, translucent red color (it should be about the same shade as raw beef). Never overcook tuna, as it will lose its moisture and delicate flavor and become dry and unappetizing. Always remove it from the heat while it is still pink in the middle. To check, slice a piece and look inside.

Seared coriander-crusted tuna steaks with miso

This is a bit of a cheat's dish, using packaged miso paste, but it's also healthy and tasty! Make sure the tuna is at room temperature before cooking, or the center will take longer to reach the correct temperature than the outside, while the outside overcooks and ruins the steak.

Serves 1 large portion, or 2 light lunches
Preparation time 15 minutes
Cooking time 10–15 minutes

1 tbsp finely crushed coriander seeds
1 tsp crushed sea salt
1 tuna steak (8½oz)
1 tbsp olive oil
1 × 1oz package miso soup paste
5½oz fresh noodles
1 tsp finely chopped fresh ginger
1 red chile, seeded and finely sliced
   on the diagonal
2 scallions, finely sliced on the diagonal
1 tbsp purple basil, finely chopped
1 tbsp cilantro
drizzle of sesame oil
1 lime, cut into wedges

1 Mix the crushed coriander and salt together, then tip onto a plate. Lay the tuna on top and push down gently, then turn over and coat the other side too.

2 Pour the oil into a skillet over medium-high heat, add the tuna and cook for about 3 minutes on each side, until lightly golden. Remove from the heat and let the tuna rest in the pan for 5–10 minutes.

3 Meanwhile, tip the miso paste into a pan and add 1¾ cups boiling water, mixing well. Place over medium heat until bubbling. Add the noodles and reduce the heat to a simmer. Tip in the ginger, chile, scallions, and purple basil.

4 Ladle the noodles and some of the soup into a large, shallow bowl. Slice the tuna and arrange on top of the noodles. Ladle more of the soup over and sprinkle with the cilantro leaves and sesame oil. Serve immediately with the lime to squeeze over just before eating.

The mysteries of miso

Miso is a fermented paste of soya beans that is an essential ingredient of Japanese food. It makes a wonderful pantry ingredient as it's delicious and takes only seconds to mix. Try your own adaptations of the dish above, by adding spinach, baby sweet corn, or sugarsnap peas, but don't overcomplicate it as you want the fresh, clean taste of the soup itself to be the star. Miso doesn't need salt, so go easy on the seasoning.

Smoked haddock fish cakes

These fish cakes can be prepared ahead of time and chilled in the refrigerator until use. This will firm them up and prevent them from breaking while cooking. Use any other sustainable smoked flaky white fish if haddock is unavailable. To make the mixture ultra-smooth, pass the cooked potato through a potato ricer, or push through a strainer.

Makes 16 small fish cakes
Preparation time 30 minutes,
   plus 30 minutes chilling
Cooking time 30 minutes
Can be made in advance to end of step 4
Suitable for freezing at end of step 4

1lb Yukon Gold potatoes, cut into 1in dice
sea salt and black pepper
1 cup milk
½lb smoked haddock or other flaky
   white fish fillets
1 bay leaf
3 tbsp olive oil
1 large onion, finely chopped
finely grated zest of 1 small lemon
   (about 2 tsp)
1 tsp paprika
½ cup plus 1 tbsp bread crumbs
2 tbsp finely chopped flat leaf parsley
4–6 tbsp all-purpose flour
2 eggs, beaten
3 tsp grainy mustard
2 tbsp half-fat crème fraîche
½lb curly kale (3 cups)

1 Put the potatoes in a pan of lightly salted water, place over high heat, and bring to a boil. Reduce the heat, cover, and simmer for 15–20 minutes, or until tender. Drain well and mash until smooth (*see* secret, page 20).

2 Pour the milk into a shallow sauté pan, add the haddock fillets and bay leaf, then season with salt and pepper. Place over low heat and bring to a simmer. Cook gently for 6–10 minutes, until the fish is separating into flakes. Carefully strain off and reserve the milk and bay leaf, cover, and set aside in the refrigerator. Flake the fish into a bowl, removing and discarding the skin and any small bones.

3 Meanwhile, pour 1 tbsp of the oil into a skillet over medium heat and gently fry together the onion, lemon zest, and paprika for 4–5 minutes, until the onion is soft but not colored. Add this to the bowl with the fish. Stir in the mashed potato and mix. Taste and add salt and pepper if necessary. Form the mixture into 16 equal-size balls, then slightly flatten them into fish cakes, each about ¾in thick.

4 Mix together the bread crumbs and parsley and season with salt and pepper. Using the bread crumbs, flour, and eggs, coat the fish cakes in a bread crumb crust (*see* secret, opposite, for how to do this). Once they are coated, cover the fish cakes with plastic wrap and refrigerate for at least 30 minutes, longer if possible: ideally make them in the morning and refrigerate until supper.

5 Remove the fish cakes from the refrigerator and return to room temperature. Preheat the oven to 350°F.

Applying a bread crumb coating to fish or meat

Make sure you have four plates close at hand: one holding flour seasoned with salt and pepper, another beaten egg, and the third bread crumbs. Leave the last empty. Dip the fish cakes, fish, or meat into the flour, shake off the excess, then turn them through the egg. Finally, press all sides into the bread crumbs. Put the coated item on the fourth plate. If you can, use just one hand for this process, to avoid getting too messy.

6 Pour the remaining oil into an ovenproof skillet, place over medium heat, then gently fry the fish cakes for 3–5 minutes on each side, until lovely and golden. Transfer the pan to the oven and cook for 10–15 minutes more.

7 Bring a pan of water that fits your steamer to a boil over high heat. Meanwhile, make the sauce. Heat the reserved milk and bay leaf in a small saucepan over medium heat. Whisk in the grainy mustard, then add the crème fraîche and allow to foam. Reduce the heat and keep the sauce warm. Place the kale in a steamer over boiling water, cover and cook for 6–8 minutes, until tender.

8 Serve the fish cakes on warmed plates with the curly kale and a large spoonful of the mustard sauce.

Thai red curry

This dish is equally delicious with chicken thighs instead of shrimp; add them with the butternut squash. When using coconut milk, whisk it briskly with a fork in the can before using—this helps to stop it splitting.

Serves 4 for a children's supper
Preparation time 20 minutes
Cooking time 40 minutes
Can be made in advance to end of step 2

1 onion, quartered
1 garlic clove
3 tbsp red curry paste
1 tbsp oil
1 × 14.5oz can chopped tomatoes
2 × 13.5oz cans coconut milk
1 cup plus 2 tbsp good fish or chicken stock
1 butternut squash (about 1lb), peeled and
    cut into ¾in dice
⅓lb sugarsnap peas
12 button mushrooms, halved
4 tbsp fish sauce, or to taste
sea salt and black pepper
12 raw jumbo shrimp, shelled and deveined
juice of 1 lime (about 2 tbsp)

For the steamed rice
1 cup basmati rice
1 cardamom pod, crushed
1 star anise

1 Place the onion, garlic, and curry paste into a food processor and blend to make a paste. If you don't have a processor, finely chop the onion and garlic together and stir in the curry paste.

2 Pour the oil into a large, deep pan and place over medium heat. When the oil is hot, add the paste with the tomatoes and cook for 5–10 minutes, stirring constantly. Add the coconut milk and stock and bring to a bubble, then reduce the heat and stir in the squash. Simmer for 10–15 minutes, or until the squash is tender. Add the sugarsnap peas and mushrooms, then gradually add the fish sauce: stir through about half, then taste and add more if you want. Season with salt and pepper to taste.

3 Meanwhile, prepare the rice. Place it in a fine-mesh strainer and rinse under cold water. Shake off the water and place the rice in a saucepan. Add 1¾-cup of cold water, a little salt, the cardamom, and star anise. Bring to a boil over high heat and cook for 5 minutes. Cover with a tight-fitting lid, reduce the heat to its lowest setting and cook for 12–14 minutes. Turn off the heat and allow to steam, still covered, for 10 minutes more.

4 Add the shrimp to the curry sauce and stir for up to 5 minutes, or until they are pink and cooked through. Taste and add salt and pepper, if necessary, and lime juice to taste. Remove the cardamom and star anise from the rice and fluff it up with a fork.

5 Serve the curry on a bed of rice.

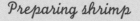

Preparing shrimp
Shrimp are sold fresh and frozen; make sure frozen shrimp are thoroughly defrosted before cooking. Remove the shell, and devein the shrimp by running a small, sharp knife carefully down the back of the shrimp, then use the knife to pull out the string.

Crab & sweet corn soup

If fresh crab meat is not available, you can easily substitute canned white crab meat. I use frozen corn here as I find it much crunchier than canned when it's cooked, which gives a good, definite texture to this aromatic, unusual soup.

Serves 4
Preparation time 10–15 minutes
Cooking time 20 minutes

4½ cups chicken stock
1 × 16oz bag frozen sweet corn
4 scallions, finely chopped
½in piece fresh ginger, peeled and
    finely chopped
1 tbsp Chinese rice wine
2–3 tsp soy sauce
1 tsp light brown sugar
2 tsp cornstarch
8oz cooked white crab meat
1 egg white
1 tsp sesame oil
shrimp crackers, to serve

1 Place the stock in a large pot and bring to a boil over high heat. Add the sweet corn, reduce the heat, and allow to simmer for 10–15 minutes. Add the scallions, ginger, rice wine, soy sauce, and sugar. In a small bowl, mix the cornstarch with just enough cold water to make a paste, then whisk this into the soup. Simmer gently, stirring, for 2–3 minutes, until the soup begins to thicken, then add the crab meat and stir.

2 In a small bowl, whisk together the egg white and sesame oil, then slowly pour this into the soup (make sure the soup is not boiling at this point), whisking constantly. It will form silky strands.

3 Serve the soup accompanied by shrimp crackers.

Tackling a whole cooked crab

Lay the crab on its back and twist off the big claws. Pull the underside of the body from the top shell. You will see a circle of gray feathery gills—pull these off and discard them. Then, using a heavy knife, cut the body into four quarters. This exposes tunnels containing the white meat. Pick it out with a skewer. Pull the knuckles from the large claws and pick out the meat. Place the large claws on a worktop and cover with a clean kitchen towel. Smash with a rolling pin until the shell cracks, then extract the meat, discarding the thin blade within each claw. Spread out all the white crab meat on a broad plate and carefully pick through it with your fingers, discarding any bits of shell you find. Spoon the brown meat from the upper shell and keep it separate from the white meat. You do not need the brown meat for this dish, but it is delicious and great in soups, tarts, turnovers, and pâtés.

Sautéed calamari with chorizo & peppers

I ate a dish similar to this one in South Africa and it was so delicious I invented my own version at home. My children had previously thought all calamari came in battered rings, but they love this. The chorizo complements the dish wonderfully (see secret, page 75).

Serves 4
Preparation time 20 minutes,
   plus 30 minutes marinating
Cooking time 10 minutes

2lb fresh calamari, cleaned and cut
   into ¾in pieces (*see* secret, below)
1 cup milk
1 tbsp olive oil
2 garlic cloves, finely chopped
1 chile, seeded and finely chopped
¼lb chorizo, diced
1 × 12oz jar roasted red peppers, drained
   and sliced
juice of ½ lemon (about 1½ tbsp)
1–2 tbsp all-purpose flour
sea salt and black pepper
2 handfuls of flatleaf parsley leaves,
   roughly chopped

1 Place the calamari into a shallow dish, pour in just enough milk to cover, cover in plastic wrap, and chill in the refrigerator for up to 30 minutes.

2 Heat the oil in a large, deep skillet over medium heat and sauté the garlic and chile for 1 minute. Add the chorizo and continue to cook for 4–5 minutes more, until it releases its oil. Add the peppers and stir for 3–4 minutes, then pour off any excess oil and add the lemon juice.

3 Meanwhile, remove the calamari from the milk and place on paper towels, to absorb any excess moisture. Put the flour in a resealable plastic bag with plenty of salt and pepper, drop in the calamari, seal the bag and shake well to coat. Pour into a strainer to remove any excess flour.

4 Add the calamari to the pan and continue to cook for just 1–2 minutes, stirring. Do not cook for any longer (*see* secret, below). Stir in the parsley, season with salt and pepper, and serve immediately.

Tackling squid

You can usually buy squid already cleaned, but if yours aren't, don't worry. Working over a sink, pull the tentacles from the body and remove and discard the plastic-like tube (the quill) that emerges from inside, along with any intestines. Tear the fins from larger squid and peel off any mottled purple-brown skin. Cut off and discard the eyes and beak from below the tentacles. Rinse the pieces under cold water, then pat dry with paper towels. To tenderize squid, soak it in milk for up to 30 minutes, then either cook for the shortest possible time over high heat or braise very slowly for more than 1 hour to break down the fibers.

Mussels with Belgian beer

Nothing is more associated with Belgium than mussels, so do the country justice and use their excellent beer in this recipe! A new twist on that old favorite moules marinière, this dish is best served with lots of crusty bread to soak up the fabulous juices.

Serves 2
Preparation time 10 minutes
Cooking time 10 minutes

1lb 2oz mussels
1 tbsp olive oil
3½oz pancetta, cubed, or bacon
1 large leek, sliced into rings
2 thyme sprigs
11oz bottle Belgian beer, such as Stella
   Artois, or other good lager

1 Clean the mussels and discard any that do not close when they are tapped on the side of the sink (*see* secret, below).

2 Pour the oil into a pan large enough to hold all the mussels and with a tight-fitting lid. Place it over medium heat and gently fry the pancetta and leek for 2–3 minutes, then add the thyme and stir until everything is cooked through.

3 Tip in the mussels and add the beer. Place the lid on the pan and leave to steam for 5 minutes, or until the mussels are open. Discard any mussels that have failed to open. Serve immediately.

How to prepare mussels

Empty the mussels into the kitchen sink, then pull off the beard (the protruding scraps of hairs) from each shell. Scrub to clean and remove the worst of any barnacles. As you work, discard any mussels that are cracked, or that are open and do not close when tapped on the side of the sink (they may be dead). Rinse in fresh water. After cooking, discard any mussels that remain closed.

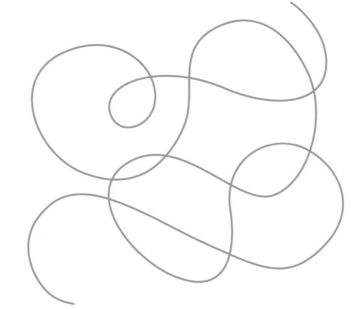

Pasta, rice, & grains

Beef & eggplant rigatoni bake with tomato & basil

Anchovy, tomato, & bacon pasta sauce · Pasta with bacon & vegetable sauce

Simple salmon, dill, & crème fraîche pasta · Haddock & spring vegetable risotto

Chicken, lemon, & arugula risotto · Red rice salad

Healthy couscous, my style

Secrets of cooking pasta, rice, & grains

You must always have dried pasta in the pantry for emergency suppers. We have spaghetti, linguine, and lasagna sheets as well as shapes such as rigatoni for my Beef & Eggplant Rigatoni Bake with Tomato & Basil (*see* page 104).

Don't just reach for the sandwiches when children need a packed lunch. Pasta, tuna, and sweet corn provides a great lunchtime energy burst for them, as does a helping of the quite fabulous, nutty Red Rice Salad (*see* page 116), which is my mother's recipe.

Always make sure your pantry includes a couple of jars of pesto and your refrigerator a hunk of Parmesan, for those nights when you haven't had time to get to the market. That way, within 10 minutes of coming through the door, you can have dinner on the table. No one ever complains that they don't like pasta, even other people's children!

As well as being a great comfort food, a dish of risotto can be a canny way to use up leftover vegetables. Once your rice is right, you can throw anything in for an easy supper. Risotto is a hands-on dish and you'll have to watch it cooking and stir, but done simply it's always a hit. Butternut squash risotto is a favorite of mine—try it!

Even if you've never tried couscous, give it a whirl. I adore it. It miraculously absorbs any sauce that surrounds it, and puffs itself up to a wonderful fluffy cloud. Try my Healthy Couscous (*see* page 118) with a dish of roasted vegetables for a simple vegetarian meal.

Beef & eggplant rigatoni bake with tomato & basil

I found it hard to persuade my children to eat eggplant, so I came up with this dish that breaks it down to mix smoothly with two of their favorite things: pasta and ground meat. The key is not to overcook the rigatoni, as it will continue to cook in the oven, so boil it only until slightly firm to the bite (or al dente), then stop cooking immediately and drain.

Serves 4–6
Preparation time 15 minutes
Cooking time 1 hour
Can be made in advance

2 eggplant, cut lengthwise into
   ½in slices
sea salt and black pepper
10½oz rigatoni
3 tbsp olive oil, plus extra for the dish
1 onion, finely chopped
1 red chile, seeded and finely chopped
2 garlic cloves, finely chopped
1lb 2oz lean ground beef
3 tbsp tomato puree
2 tbsp Worcestershire sauce
2 × 14.5oz cans chopped tomatoes
handful of basil leaves, finely chopped
2½ cups low-fat cottage cheese,
   drained
½ cup finely grated Parmesan cheese
4½oz ball of mozzarella cheese, sliced

Which pasta shape?

Rigatoni is ideal for this dish, as the chunky sauce clings to the ribbed tubes. If you're out of rigatoni, substitute another pasta of a similar shape, such as penne. (In the same way, the tagliatelle I use with my Anchovy, Tomato, & Bacon Pasta Sauce—see page 107—can be substituted with similar-shaped linguine or spaghetti.)

1 Put the eggplant slices in a colander, sprinkle with plenty of salt and stand the colander over a bowl for 15–20 minutes to draw the water from the eggplant.

2 Bring a large pan of salted water to a boil and cook the pasta for 8–10 minutes, or according to package instructions, until *al dente*. Drain, drizzle with 1 tbsp of the oil, season with salt and pepper, and toss. Set aside.

3 Heat another 1 tbsp of the oil in a sauté pan over medium heat and cook the onion, chile, and garlic for 2–3 minutes, stirring. Add the ground beef and cook for another 5–6 minutes, until it is browned all over. Add the tomato puree and Worcestershire sauce, season with salt and pepper, then add the tomatoes and basil. Reduce the heat and simmer for 20 minutes. Preheat the oven to 375°F.

4 Meanwhile, rinse the salt from the eggplant slices and pat dry with paper towels. Pour the remaining oil into a large nonstick skillet or griddle placed over high heat, and fry the eggplant for 1–2 minutes on each side until golden brown. You may need to do this in batches.

5 Lightly oil a deep 8½ × 11in ovenproof dish. Lay a third of the eggplant into the dish, then spread over half the pasta. Add half the cottage cheese, then half the ground beef and a third of the Parmesan. Repeat the layers, then finish with the remaining eggplant slices and Parmesan. Arrange the mozzarella evenly over the top. Bake for 30 minutes, until bubbling around the sides. Serve hot.

Anchovy, tomato, & bacon pasta sauce

This is a great from-the-pantry recipe. You can substitute dried pasta for the fresh tagliatelle used here, but remember it will double in volume once cooked. This is a little like the Italian puttanesca sauce, though I have omitted the olives—my children find them overpowering—and added bacon. Rinsed capers would go nicely in this as well; use 1 tablespoon if you like them.

Serves 4 hungry children
Preparation time 10 minutes
Cooking time 30 minutes
Can be made in advance to end of step 2

2 tbsp olive oil
1 garlic clove, finely chopped
1 large onion, finely sliced
5oz bacon or pancetta, sliced
4oz can anchovies in olive oil, drained
2 × 14.5oz cans chopped tomatoes
handful of basil leaves, roughly chopped
2 tbsp Worcestershire sauce
sea salt and black pepper
1lb 2oz fresh tagliatelle
lots of freshly grated Parmesan cheese

1 Heat half the oil in a large skillet over low to medium heat. Add the garlic and onion and gently fry, stirring, until softened, then add the bacon or pancetta and fry until golden. Add the anchovies to the skillet, cooking to allow them to break up slightly.

2 Stir the tomatoes into the pan, add the basil and Worcestershire sauce and season with salt and pepper. Mix well and allow to simmer and thicken for at least 25 minutes. The longer you can leave the sauce to simmer, the better. Stir occasionally so it doesn't stick on the bottom of the pan.

3 Bring a large saucepan of salted water to boil and cook the pasta according to package instructions, until *al dente*. Drain, drizzle with the remaining oil, grind some black pepper on top and toss.

4 Divide the pasta between 4 warmed serving bowls, and spoon the sauce over. Serve with a generous sprinkle of Parmesan.

Cooking perfect pasta
Use a very large saucepan filled with boiling water and stir for the first minute of cooking. Always salt the water as this will enhance the flavor of the pasta. If your pan is too small or contains too little water, the pasta will stick and clump together and cook unevenly. Once you add the pasta to the pan, adjust the heat so the water doesn't boil up and spill over the sides. Most dried pasta cooks in about 8–12 minutes, but always test a piece to ensure it is tender though slightly firm to the bite (*al dente*) before draining.

Pasta with bacon & vegetable sauce

To give this dish a simple twist, omit the tomatoes and stir in a couple of spoonfuls of pesto 5 minutes before the sauce is ready (store-bought pesto is fine!).

Serves 4
Preparation time 15 minutes
Cooking time 30 minutes
Can be made in advance to end of step 1

2 tbsp olive oil
scant ¾ cup fresh bread crumbs
¼ cup finely grated Parmesan cheese
2 tbsp finely chopped basil leaves,
    plus extra to garnish
14oz spaghetti

For the sauce
1 tbsp olive oil
1 red onion, finely chopped
1 red chile, seeded and finely chopped
1 garlic clove, finely chopped
1 zucchini, cut into half moons
1 small eggplant, diced
8 slices bacon, chopped
14.5oz can whole tomatoes
12 button mushrooms, halved
small handful of basil leaves
sea salt and black pepper

1 First make the sauce. Pour the oil into a large saucepan over medium heat and add the onion, chile, and garlic. Fry gently for 5 minutes, until the onion has softened but not browned. Add the zucchini, eggplant, and bacon and cook for 15 minutes, or until the vegetables are tender. Stir in the tomatoes, mushrooms, and basil, taste and season with salt and a generous amount of pepper. Simmer for 10 minutes more.

2 Bring a large pan of salted water to a boil over high heat, adding ½ tbsp of the oil. Meanwhile, pour 1 tbsp of the oil into a small skillet over high heat and toss in the bread crumbs, stirring constantly until they are toasted a light golden brown. Remove from the heat and mix in the Parmesan and basil. Set aside.

3 Cook the spaghetti in the saucepan of boiling water, following the package instructions, until *al dente*. Drain, drizzle in the remaining oil, grind over more black pepper, and toss.

4 Serve the spaghetti in warmed serving bowls and spoon the sauce over the top, then sprinkle on the toasted bread crumbs and garnish with a little chopped basil.

Pasta: fresh or dried?

Fresh and dried pasta have different roles in the kitchen: generally speaking, dried pasta is firmer when cooked and suits chunkier, oilier, often meat-based sauces. It is cheaper and keeps very well. Fresh pasta is better suited to creamy sauces and those with a more delicate flavor.

Simple salmon, dill, & crème fraîche pasta

This recipe is so easy. Take care with dill; it is a delicious herb but is also quite strong and you don't want it to overpower the dish. The whole plate should have a delicate tang and be sparkling with subtle flavors.

Serves 4
Preparation time 5–10 minutes
Cooking time 15–20 minutes

4 salmon fillets (about 5oz each)
sea salt and black pepper
2 tbsp olive oil
10½oz spaghetti, preferably fresh
½ tbsp fresh dill, finely chopped
zest of 1 lemon (about 3 tsp)
juice of 1 lemon (about 3 tbsp)
4–6 tbsp crème fraîche

1 Preheat the oven to 375°F.

2 Place the salmon fillets in an ovenproof dish, season with salt and pepper, and drizzle with half the oil, turning the fillets to coat all sides. Roast in the oven for 10–15 minutes, until the salmon is very moist and still slightly pink in the middle (slice off a chunk to check).

3 Bring a large pan of salted water to a boil over high heat and cook the pasta according to the package instructions until *al dente*. Drain, return to the pan, and toss with the remaining oil to prevent it from sticking.

4 Meanwhile, flake the salmon into a bowl and toss with the dill and lemon zest. Add to the pasta and gently mix through with the lemon juice and crème fraîche, keeping the fish in large flakes. Season well with salt and pepper and serve immediately.

Perfect fish with pasta

When you cook any pasta recipe containing fish, be very sure not to overcook the fish. It needs to remain slightly underdone, as its residual heat combined with the piping hot pasta will continue to cook it when it is added to the sauce. So make sure that it has a faint translucent quality in the center before you add it to pasta, which indicates that it is slightly undercooked.

Haddock & spring vegetable risotto

For a slightly healthier version, use half-fat crème fraîche instead of butter. I double-blanch the rice for risottos. You may think this makes it a laborious process, but you'll find that it removes some of the starch and produces a lighter dish while cutting down on the the cooking time.

Serves 4
Preparation time 15 minutes
Cooking time 30 minutes

10½oz smoked haddock or other flaky
   white fish fillets, skin on
1 cup milk
2 cups fish or vegetable stock
2 bay leaves
2 rosemary sprigs
1½ cups risotto rice
1 tbsp olive oil
4 baby zucchini, cut into ½in slices
6 asparagus spears, cut into ½in slices
3 scallions, finely chopped
½ tbsp butter
3 tbsp finely grated Parmesan cheese
finely grated zest of 1 lime (about 1 tsp)
juice of 1 lime (about 2 tbsp)
small handful of mint leaves, chopped,
   to serve (optional)

1 Lay the haddock in a saucepan and cover with the milk and 1 cup of the stock, adding the bay leaves and rosemary. Place over medium heat and bring to a boil, then turn off the heat and allow the fish to cool in the liquid.

2 Meanwhile, bring a pan of water to a boil over high heat and pour in the rice. Boil for 2–3 minutes, then drain. Put the rice back into the rinsed-out saucepan, cover with cold water and bring up to a boil again. Simmer for 3–4 minutes, then pour into a fine-mesh strainer and rinse under cold water to stop it cooking any more.

3 Lift the haddock from the cooking liquid and remove the skin. Strain the cooking liquid and set aside. Flake the haddock, removing as many bones as you can. Set aside.

4 Heat the oil in a large pan, add the risotto rice and stir to coat all the grains. Add a couple of ladles of the reserved haddock liquid, stir and allow it all to be absorbed. Then add a little more, stirring, each time allowing the liquid to be absorbed before adding more, and using as much of the remaining stock as you need. After about 10 minutes of this, add the zucchini and asparagus.

5 Taste the rice; when it's ready it should be *al dente*. Add the scallions and flaked haddock, gently stir through, then add the butter to thicken the risotto and give it a gloss. Add the Parmesan and keep stirring: you will see the last of the liquid thicken. Add in the lime zest and juice. Serve in warmed bowls and sprinkle each portion with mint, if you like.

The wonders of poaching liquid

Never throw away the liquid used for poaching fish. It will contribute to your final dish, making a wonderful stock or sauce. Here it brings fishy, herby flavors to the risotto. For a quick dish, poach a fish fillet, keep it warm while you boil down the poaching liquor to intensify its flavors, then whisk in butter to thicken. A great, speedy sauce!

Chicken, lemon, & arugula risotto

Citrus and slightly spicy arugula make this quick, easy dish delicious. Risotto is a hands-on dish—you can't just leave it on the stove—so I tend to make it when the children can sit at the kitchen table at the same time and we go through their spelling homework.

Serves 4 children
Preparation time 10 minutes
Cooking time 45 minutes

4 cups good-quality chicken stock
2 skinless, boneless chicken breasts
3 tbsp unsalted butter
1 red onion, finely chopped
²/₃ cup risotto rice
½ cup dry white wine
½ cup arugula leaves
finely grated zest of 1 lemon (about 3 tsp)
1½oz Parmesan cheese, shaved
sea salt and black pepper

1 Place the chicken stock into a large saucepan and bring to a boil over high heat. Reduce to a simmer and add the chicken breasts. Poach for 10 minutes, then remove a breast to a plate and slice it through. If there is any trace of pink, return the breast to the pan for 2 minutes more, then check it again. Remove the chicken from the pan with a slotted spoon and slice into bite-size pieces. Keep the stock hot over low heat.

2 Put 2tbsp of the butter in a sauté pan or deep skillet and melt over low heat. Add the onion, fry gently until soft, then add the rice and stir gently for 2 minutes. Pour in the wine, allow most of it to be absorbed, then ladle in some of the hot chicken stock and stir until that, too, is absorbed. Continue to add ladles of hot stock to the rice, stirring gently and allowing the stock to be absorbed between each addition, for about 18 minutes, or until the rice is cooked but still *al dente*.

3 Five minutes before the rice is cooked, stir in the chicken slices, arugula, lemon zest, remaining butter, and Parmesan. Heat through thoroughly. Taste and add salt and pepper, if necessary, and serve.

The secret of risotto

You must use short-grained risotto rice when cooking risotto; it has a high starch content, which produces a creamy texture. The most common type is arborio. Gradually adding hot stock, waiting until each ladle is absorbed before adding the next, and stirring constantly, are the keys to the dish. Stirring in butter and Parmesan at the end of cooking, and leaving for 5 minutes before serving will give a creamier finish. Be careful not to overcook the rice as the grains should remain slightly firm to the bite. The overall texture of the finished dish should be gorgeously unctuous and it shouldn't separate into a pile of rice surrounded by a moat of liquid. The Italians have the best phrase for it—*all'onda*, which means the risotto should form "waves" on the plate if you tip it.

Red rice salad

Camargue red rice is a special variety grown only in the south of France. I think it is best used for light salads as it is bulkier than white rice and has a nutty flavor that is complemented by a light dressing. Look for it in gourmet shops or substitute a combination of brown and wild rice.

Serves 4
Preparation time 15 minutes
Cooking time 25 minutes
Can be made in advance

1 cup Camargue red rice
2 tbsp olive oil, plus extra to drizzle
1 red chile, seeded and finely chopped
20 jumbo shrimp, uncooked, peeled and
    deveined (*see* secret, page 92)
sea salt and black pepper
10 basil leaves, finely sliced
3 scallions, finely chopped
4 sun-dried tomatoes, thinly sliced
3 tbsp finely chopped flatleaf parsley

For the dressing
3 tbsp olive oil
1 tbsp grainy mustard
zest of 1 lemon (about 3 tsp), finely grated
juice of 1 lemon (about 3 tbsp)

1 Cook the rice according to the package instructions. Drain and refresh under cold running water. Drizzle a little oil over to ensure it does not clump together. Set aside.

2 Meanwhile, pour the 2 tbsp oil into a skillet and place over medium heat until hot. Add the chile and shrimp, season with salt and pepper and fry gently for 4–5 minutes until the shrimp are cooked through and nicely pink. Toss in the basil toward the end of cooking. Remove from the heat and let cool.

3 Pour the rice into a large bowl, stir in the scallions, sun-dried tomatoes, parsley, and cooled shrimp mixture. Toss together.

4 Mix together all the ingredients for the dressing and add a pinch each of salt and pepper. Stir the dressing well into the rice salad—be generous with it and allow it to absorb into the rice before serving.

Cooking a perfect pan of rice

Many experienced cooks struggle to make fluffy rice. To achieve it with white rice, measure out the amount you need in a measuring cup. Note the volume, then pour into a pan, adding double the amount of water. Bring to a simmer, cover and cook for 15 minutes, or according to the package instructions. Remove from the heat, place a clean kitchen towel under the lid and leave for 5 minutes. Fluff up with a fork before serving.

Healthy couscous, my style

This is the perfect accompaniment to meat (it's ideal with my Indian Lamb Chops, see page 46), or simply serve it as a light salad on its own. Couscous has a fabulous ability to soak up any sauce that surrounds it, so it's a great alternative to rice or mashed potatoes.

Serves 6
Preparation time 10–15 minutes

1 cup couscous
olive oil, to drizzle
4 preserved lemons, flesh discarded,
   zest finely chopped
1/3 cup golden raisins
1/4 cup sliced almonds, toasted
1 tbsp finely chopped mint leaves
1 tbsp finely chopped cilantro leaves
sea salt and black pepper

1 Prepare the couscous (*see* secret, below), adding 1¼ cups boiling water.

2 Simply add all the other ingredients to the couscous, seasoning well with salt and pepper, and mix together.

How to prepare couscous
Pour the couscous into a large heatproof bowl and add boiling water, using a ratio of 4 parts couscous to 5 parts boiling water. Add a little oil, fork it through, then cover with plastic wrap. Leave for 5–10 minutes. When the couscous has absorbed the liquid, separate the grains, being careful to remove any clumps with a fork, if necessary adding a little more oil. Cover and leave for another 10 minutes.

Pies, pastries, tarts, & batters

Classic ham hock pot pie · Bacon, mushroom, & cheese pastry parcels

Ricotta, pepper, & artichoke quiche · Pissaladière · Breakfast rolls

Shrimp, chorizo, & baby zucchini tempura

Impressively pretty fruit tarts · Remarkably easy pastry cream

Homemade sweet shortcrust pastry · Traditional treacle tart

Pineapple tarte tatin · Fresh cherry jam tart · Phyllo lemon tart

Secrets of cooking pies, pastries, tarts, & batters

Pot pies are a treat in our home, as I don't make them often, but all the family love them. They are a great idea when you have some leftover chicken and bottom-of-the-refrigerator vegetables that have to be eaten.

I have given a recipe for Classic Ham Hock Pot Pie (*see* page 124). We have an amazing butcher and he's very generous with his advice if I want to do something different. He suggested this pie, which is now part of my repertoire as it's deeply comforting, hearty, and a bit indulgent. It's not for those watching their figure, but I can't think of a better meal for a winter's night.

When we were photographing recipes for this book, I had a perfect moment when we prepared the Impressively Pretty Fruit Tarts (*see* page 138). Just as they were ready, the kids came in from school and all 8 of their eyes were popped out! That recipe is best for when you've got a bit of time, but always makes a real impact. I will cook them if my mother-in-law is coming to visit, to make a good impression! They are great fun to cook and really easy.

In my time, I have bought two deep-fryers and I have always ended up hating them. You can never clean them properly. Now, I deep-fry my Shrimp, Chorizo, & Baby Zucchini Tempura (*see* page 135) in a pan over the stove. Take care, though; you have got to be incredibly wary as oil at that temperature is very unforgiving. Always have your pan on the back of the stove. Send the kids out of the kitchen. Have paper towels on the side ready to blot off any excess oil from your fried items. And respect it. Leave the pan to cool down completely and save any old bottles to dispose of the oil.

I love quiche and have no time for those people who say it's old-fashioned. My Ricotta, Pepper, & Artichoke Quiche (*see* page 130) is amazing. It is really easy to pull together using ingredients from the refrigerator and pantry. If you have vegetarians for lunch (not Gordon's favorite guests!), it's easy to make two quiches, one meat-free—with a salad and my Best-ever Homemade Fries (*see* page 164)—so everyone's happy.

Classic ham hock pot pie

Puff pastry is the traditional topping for chicken and beef pot pies. Try it with ham—as I do here—or even fish. It goes very well with creamy—and especially cheesy—sauces. Press the tines of a fork evenly around the edge of the pastry lid both to seal and decorate.

Serves 4–6
Preparation time 30 minutes
Cooking time 3¼ hours
Can be made in advance
Suitable for freezing at end of step 5

3lb 3oz ham hock
5 garlic cloves, smashed with the
    heel of the hand
5 thyme sprigs
1 leek, halved lengthwise
1 onion, quartered
1 carrot, halved lengthwise

For the pie
1 turnip, cut into ½in dice
4 carrots, cut into ½in dice
4 tbsp butter
¼ cup flour, plus extra to dust
3 tbsp heavy cream
3 tbsp chopped flatleaf parsley
sea salt and black pepper
13oz prepared puff pastry sheets
1 egg yolk, beaten

Covering a baking dish
Once you have rolled out the pastry, it's important to seal the pie properly. Choose a dish with a flat rim to it, and brush the rim with either water or egg yolk, then stick on a strip of pastry trimmings. Wrap the pastry loosely around the rolling pin and lay it over the dish. Press it onto the rim with your fingers, crimping or pressing with a fork all the way round.

1 Place the hock in a large pan with the garlic, thyme, leek, onion, and carrot. Pour in enough cold water to cover and place over medium-high heat. Bring to a boil, reduce the heat to a simmer, cover and cook for 2½ hours. It is ready when the meat falls easily from the bone.

2 Toward the end of the cooking time, bring a pan of water to a boil and drop in the turnip and carrots for 5 minutes, until they are just slightly underdone. Drain and set aside.

3 When it is cool enough to handle, remove the ham from its stock and pull the meat from the bone in large bite-size pieces. Discard the bone and skin. Put the ham into an 11 × 7in ovenproof baking dish. Strain the vegetables and herbs from the delicious stock. Preheat the oven to 400°F.

4 Melt the butter over gentle heat and, when it is bubbling, stir in the flour until it absorbs all the butter and dries out slightly. Gradually whisk in 2¼ cups of the stock until the sauce thickens, then add the cream and parsley and season with salt and pepper.

5 Put the turnip and carrot into the baking dish and pour over the sauce. Roll out the puff pastry on a floured surface (*see* secret, page 132) and use it to cover the baking dish (*see* secret, left).

6 Brush the top of the pie with egg yolk and cook in the oven for 30 minutes, until golden brown. Serve hot.

Bacon, mushroom, & cheese pastry parcels

These turnovers are handy and very portable snacks for a picnic or children's party. They can also be adapted to make canapés or quick lunchtime snacks with the filling of your choice; you can use almost anything in them, but these are the ones my children like best.

Serves 4
Preparation time 10 minutes
Cooking time 30 minutes
Can be made in advance
Suitable for freezing at end of step 3

1 tbsp olive oil, plus extra for the
    baking sheet
4 slices of unsmoked bacon,
    preferably maple, chopped
8 button mushrooms, finely sliced
3½oz aged Cheddar cheese, grated
4 cherry tomatoes, quartered
2 tbsp chopped basil leaves
sea salt and black pepper
15oz prepared puff pastry sheet
1 egg, beaten

1 Preheat the oven to 425°F.

2 Heat the oil in a nonstick skillet over medium heat and sauté the bacon and mushrooms for 3–4 minutes, or until golden. Remove from the heat, transfer to a large bowl, and allow to cool. Add the cheese, tomatoes, and basil, season with salt and pepper, and mix.

3 Cut the pastry sheet into 4 rectangles. Spoon even quantities of the bacon mixture onto half of each rectangle, making sure you leave a ½in gap around the edges. Brush these edges with a little of the egg, then fold the other half of the pastry over to encase the filling. With floured fingers, crimp the edges to seal (*see* photographs, pages 128–9). Using a sharp knife, make small slits in the top of each parcel. Brush with the remaining egg.

4 Place on a lightly oiled baking sheet, brush with the remaining egg, and bake for 20–25 minutes until the pastry is golden brown and the cheese is slightly oozing out of the sides.

5 Serve wrapped in parchment paper to cold and hungry kids after football.

How to make a perfect turnover

Be careful not to overfill the pastry or the turnovers might break open, and remember to leave room to crimp and seal the edges. This can be done with a fork or simply with your thumb and finger. Brushing the turnovers with beaten egg before cooking helps make them glossy and golden brown.

Ricotta, pepper, & artichoke quiche

This is a great way to use up odds and ends from the refrigerator. You can vary the type of cheese you use and the vegetables you put in, according to what you have left over, but this is my favorite, and I always have marinated anchovies and artichokes around.

Serves 4–6
Preparation time 15 minutes,
    plus 1 hour chilling
Cooking time 1 hour
Can be made in advance

¼ × 12oz jar roasted peppers,
    sliced into strips
6 marinated artichokes, quartered
10 marinated anchovies
2 eggs, lightly beaten
1 cup ricotta cheese
¼ cup grated Parmesan cheese
scant ⅓ cup milk
scant ⅓ cup heavy cream
sea salt and black pepper

For the pastry
1¼ cups all-purpose flour, plus extra to dust
5½ tbsp unsalted butter,
    plus extra for the pan

1 First make the pastry. Sift the flour and a pinch of salt into a large bowl. Add the butter, cut into pieces, and rub with your fingertips until the mixture resembles bread crumbs. Add enough cold water to bring together into a firm dough, then wrap in plastic wrap and rest it in the refrigerator for 30 minutes.

2 Roll out the pastry on a floured surface and use it to line a well-buttered 8in pie pan. Chill for another 30 minutes in the refrigerator.

3 Preheat the oven to 375°F.

4 Remove the pastry shell from the fridge and blind bake for 20 minutes (*see* secret, page 142). Remove the beans and parchment and return to the oven for another 5 minutes. Set aside to cool and reduce the oven temperature to 340°F.

5 Layer the peppers, artichokes, and anchovies in the pastry shell. Whisk together all the other filling ingredients and ladle the mixture in; it should just reach the top of the pastry shell. Cook for 35–40 minutes until ready (*see* secret, below).

6 Remove the quiche from the oven and allow to rest for 10–15 minutes, then slice into wedges and serve.

A perfectly cooked quiche

Quiche should have a velvety, slightly wobbly filling, not one of hard-set rubberiness. To achieve this silky texture, make sure you do not overcook it. It **is** ready when the top is beginning to become golden brown and the middle of the quiche has a wobble to it when you shake the pan. If the center feels springy to the touch, I'm afraid you've gone too far!

Pissaladière

This is my variation on the tart I have enjoyed in the south of France. There are many arguments about what's in the classic dish—whether it has tomatoes or not, and which pastry to use—but this is the version I enjoy the most and love to eat hot or cold. If you're not keen on olives, use 1 tablespoon rinsed capers instead.

Serves 4
Preparation time 30 minutes
Cooking time 40 minutes
Can be made in advance

13oz prepared puff pastry sheets
all-purpose flour, to dust
4 tbsp olive oil, plus extra for the
  baking sheet
1 egg yolk
1 large onion, finely sliced
2 garlic cloves, crushed
4 plum tomatoes, roughly chopped
2 tbsp tomato puree
1 tsp fresh thyme leaves
black pepper
2 × 2oz cans anchovy fillets, drained
⅓ cup black olives, pitted

1 Preheat the oven to 400°F.

2 Roll out the pastry on a floured surface into a rectangle measuring about 12 × 9½in and ¼in thick. Place on a lightly oiled baking sheet and, using a sharp knife, score a border about ¾in from the edge all the way around. Brush this edge with egg yolk to help make it beautifully golden brown when cooked.

3 Heat half the oil in a large skillet over low heat and sauté the onion and garlic very slowly. They need to become very soft but not brown. Add the tomatoes and cook for 10 minutes, or until the liquid has evaporated. Add the tomato puree, thyme, and pepper to taste, stir and cook for 4–5 minutes more. Remove from the heat and allow to cool slightly.

4 Spoon the onion and tomato mixture inside the pastry border and arrange the anchovy fillets over it in a lattice formation, then arrange the olives on top and drizzle with the remaining oil. Place in the oven for 20–25 minutes, or until the pastry is puffed around the edges and golden brown.

5 Allow to cool slightly before serving, or serve at room temperature.

Rolling out pastry

It is important to have a cool work surface—away from the stove if possible—and to dust both the surface and your rolling pin with flour to stop the pastry from sticking. Take the pastry from the refrigerator and allow it to lose a little of its chill before rolling; if it is too cold it may crack. Apply gentle pressure with the rolling pin, turning the pastry occasionally for an even thickness and to prevent it from sticking to the work surface, dusting with a little more flour if needed. When using puff pastry, never re-roll trimmings as they won't rise.

Breakfast rolls

Greet the day with these delicious rolls by using merguez instead of plain pork sausages, or even adding a spoonful of curry paste. Keep them on standby in the freezer, to pull out for an emergency brunch, Sunday football fans, or when you're feeling fragile after a late night!

Serves 4
Preparation time 5–10 minutes
Cooking time 35–40 minutes
Can be made in advance
Suitable for freezing at end of step 2

4 large pork sausage links
10 slices pancetta, or bacon
13oz prepared puff pastry sheet,
    cut into 4 squares
1 egg, beaten
2 tbsp tomato puree
2 tbsp grated Parmesan cheese
sea salt

1 Tightly wrap 2 of the pork sausages in 5 slices of pancetta each. Lightly brush the edge of each pastry square with a little of the egg. Wrap each of the pancetta-wrapped sausages in a square of puff pastry, allowing the ends to poke out.

2 Spread 1 tbsp tomato puree on the remaining pastry squares, sprinkle with the Parmesan, place on a sausage and roll tightly; gently fold over the ends on these rolls to encase the cheese and tomato filling.

3 Brush each roll with beaten egg, transfer to a baking sheet lined with parchment paper and refrigerate for 20 minutes to rest the pastry. Meanwhile, preheat the oven to 350°F. Sprinkle the rolls with salt, then bake for 35–40 minutes, until golden brown.

4 Remove the rolls from the oven and allow to cool for 10–15 minutes before serving.

Pretty pastries

There are several things you can do to make these or any other pastries look really professional. Always finish with a glaze. Milk will do for ease and economy, but beaten egg will make them beautifully golden, while beaten egg yolk gives extra glossiness. Try sprinkling with poppy or sesame seeds before baking, but always check that your guests are not allergic to sesame before serving.

Shrimp, chorizo, & baby zucchini tempura

Make sure you get raw chorizo for this recipe; cooked chorizo is not suitable for deep-frying as it will become very tough indeed. These are great as an appetizer or a party nibble with my Chile & Lime Mayonnaise (see page 274).

Serves 4
Preparation time 5–10 minutes
Cooking time 10 minutes
Can be made in advance

vegetable oil, to deep-fry
all-purpose flour, to coat
16 jumbo shrimp, uncooked, peeled
    and deveined (see secret, page 92)
4 raw chorizo sausages, cut into even chunks
7oz baby zucchini, sliced lengthwise
lime wedges, to serve

For the batter
2/3 cup all-purpose flour
1 tbsp cornstarch
1/2 tsp salt
1 cup ice-cold sparkling
    mineral water
1 ice cube

1 Pour enough oil into a deep saucepan to make a layer 2in deep. Place over medium heat until the temperature on a cook's thermometer reads 356°F. If you don't have a cook's thermometer, the oil is hot enough when a cube of bread will sizzle and turn brown when dropped in.

2 To make the batter, place the flour, cornstarch, and salt into a large mixing bowl. Whisk in the water; do not over-mix but make sure it is all combined. Add the ice cube to keep it really cold.

3 Place the flour on a plate and use it to dredge the shrimp, chorizo, and zucchini, shaking off any excess. Dip the items into the batter, then carefully add each to the hot oil, standing well back. Deep-fry in batches for 2–3 minutes (see secret, below) or until crisp and golden. Carefully remove with a slotted spoon and keep warm while you cook the rest.

4 Serve with lime wedges to squeeze over.

How to deep-fry
You have to take great care when deep-frying to avoid burns and kitchen fires. Never leave the pan of hot oil unattended, and never fill a pan more than half full. Add your items in batches, taking care not to overcrowd the pan or your food will emerge soggy rather than crisp. Using a slotted spoon, turn the items once or twice so all sides brown evenly, then remove and blot excess oil on paper towels.

Impressively pretty fruit tarts

Presentation is key here. I have mentioned raspberries in the recipe, but you can choose blackberries, blueberries, or strawberries depending on the season. I find these work best as individual tarts; you will need nine 4in tart pans.

Makes nine 4in tarts
Preparation time 10 minutes,
    plus 2 hours cooling
Cooking time 17 minutes
Can be made in advance to end of step 2

1lb 2oz sweet shortcrust pastry
    (*see* page 142)
2¾ cups pastry cream (*see* page 141)
1 pint fresh raspberries
3 tbsp raspberry jam (optional)
2 tbsp confectioners' sugar (optional)

Avoid a soggy base
To keep your tart bases crisp and toothsome, bake the pastry shells as described above (first filled with dried beans, then without) to seal them and give a cookie-like crunch. Fill with the pastry cream only just before serving to minimize the risk of any soaking into the shell.

1 Preheat the oven to 350°F.

2 Roll out the pastry, use it to line the tart pans and blind bake (*see* page 142) for 12 minutes. Remove the beans and papers then return to the oven for a further 5 minutes. Allow to cool for at least 2 hours.

3 Divide the pastry cream between the pastry shells and smooth the tops.

4 Cut the raspberries in half lengthwise and arrange over the pastry cream, starting from the edge and moving into the center in a circle formation.

5 Spoon the jam (if using) into a small pan, add 1 tbsp water and place over low heat until it melts, then push through a fine-mesh strainer. Gently brush this glaze on the raspberries.

6 Alternatively, put the confectioners' sugar (if using) in a tea strainer and shake it evenly over the tarts.

Remarkably easy pastry cream

I was really worried the first time I tried this. I had previously followed recipes that sent me into complete meltdown, but here is my easy solution; and I have yet to mess it up! It's great for éclairs and tart fillings. Substitute 1 teaspoon vanilla extract if you don't have vanilla beans.

Makes 2¾ cups—enough to fill
  a 9in pastry shell
Preparation time 5 minutes,
  plus 3 hours chilling
Cooking time 15 minutes
Can be made in advance

2 cups plus 2 tbsp milk
¼ cup plus 3 tbsp superfine sugar
1 vanilla bean (optional)
5 egg yolks
2 tbsp all-purpose flour
4 tbsp (½ stick) unsalted butter

Cooking perfect pastry cream

Make sure you don't cook the cream over a high heat as it may stick at the bottom of the pan. Use a spatula and whisk, taking care to reach all the corners, and stir continuously. Be patient and, once it has thickened, strain the cream through a fine-mesh strainer. Remember it will continue to thicken while cooling. Laying a sheet of plastic wrap directly on the surface will prevent a skin from forming and leave you with lovely, silky-smooth cream—delicious!

1 Pour the milk and half the sugar into a saucepan. Slice the vanilla bean (if using) lengthwise and add it to the pan. Place over medium heat and bring to a boil, then remove from the heat.

2 Place the egg yolks and remaining sugar in a large mixing bowl and, using a handheld electric mixer, beat briskly until pale in color. Add the flour, continuing to mix.

3 Remove the vanilla bean (if using) from the hot milk, scrape out the black, sticky seeds with the point of a knife and return these to the milk. Discard the empty pod. Very slowly pour half the milk into the egg-flour mixture, mixing constantly, then pour this back into the saucepan and place it over low to medium heat. Pour in the rest of the milk, still mixing all the time.

4 From now on, I alternate between a spatula to scrape the bottom and sides of the pan to make sure none of the cream is sticking, and a whisk to whisk the cream. You will see the pastry cream thickening. Allow it to come to a boil, still stirring and whisking constantly, for no more than 1 minute, then remove from the heat and pour through a fine-mesh strainer into a cold mixing bowl. Add the butter and stir gently until melted.

5 Lay a piece of plastic wrap on the surface of the pastry cream to stop a skin from forming. Leave to cool a little, then place it in the refrigerator to chill for at least 3 hours. Now you are ready to use your homemade pastry cream—and you should be proud!

Homemade sweet shortcrust pastry

I used to buy ready-made shortcrust pastry until I forgot. Reluctantly, I had a go at making my own. I've never bought a package since. Use an electric stand mixer and dough hook to stop your hands making the dough too warm; or run your hands under cold water to cool them.

Makes about 1lb 2oz or enough
   for two 10in tarts
Preparation time 15 minutes,
   plus 45 minutes chilling
Cooking time 25 minutes
Can be made in advance
Suitable for freezing

1¾ cups all-purpose flour, plus extra to dust
¼ cup confectioners' sugar
9 tbsp cold unsalted butter,
   cut into cubes, plus extra for the pan
2 large eggs
splash of milk

Preparing a pastry shell

Follow the instructions for rolling out pastry on page 132. Loosely wrap the pastry around the rolling pin, then unroll it over a lightly buttered tart pan. Do not stretch the pastry over the pan as this will cause it to shrink during cooking. Gently press the pastry into the edges of the pan and trim off the excess. Use the trimmings to patch any holes in the shell. Prick the pastry base all over with a fork to ensure there are no air bubbles, then chill to prevent any shrinkage in the oven. Line the pan with parchment paper and fill with dried beans or uncooked rice to prevent the base from rising.

1 Sift the flour and confectioners' sugar into a large mixing bowl and add the butter cubes. Using your fingertips, rub the butter in until the mixture resembles fine bread crumbs. At this stage, either continue with your hands or transfer to an electric stand mixer fitted with a dough hook.

2 Beat together 1 of the eggs with the milk, add to the dough and mix until it just comes together into a crumbly ball. Do not overwork: it should look a little dry. Add a little more flour if needed.

3 Shape the dough into a ball, wrap it in plastic wrap and refrigerate for at least 45 minutes or up to a day.

4 It is often necessary to blind bake the pastry. To do this, remove the plastic wrap and roll the pastry out on a floured surface, using a floured rolling pin, until ¼in thick. Use it to line a lightly buttered tart pan (*see secret, left*). Cover with plastic wrap and return to the refrigerator for 30 minutes. Preheat the oven to 350°F.

5 Line the pastry with parchment paper and fill with dried beans or uncooked rice, to prevent the pastry from rising. Bake in the oven for 20 minutes, until golden brown. Remove the parchment paper and beans or rice. Beat the remaining egg, use it to brush the pastry all over, then return to the oven for another 5 minutes to seal the pastry; this stops the base becoming soggy. Remove from the oven and allow to cool before filling.

Traditional treacle tart

This is the kind of dessert I love, but I keep it for special occasions! It needs a little advance planning, as the filling is best made the day before and the pastry needs time in the refrigerator. But, after that's done, it is an easy dessert to put together on a busy entertaining day. This is delicious served with a large dollop of crème fraîche.

Serves 8
Preparation time 15 minutes,
   plus overnight chilling
Cooking time 45 minutes
Can be made in advance to end of step 2

¼ cup ground almonds
finely grated zest of 1 orange
   (about 1½ tbsp)
⅓ cup fresh white bread crumbs
1½ cups dark corn syrup
½ cup plus 1 tbsp heavy cream
1 large egg
butter for the pan
12oz sweet shortcrust pastry
   (*see* opposite)

1 Mix the almonds, orange zest, and bread crumbs in a large bowl. Spoon the corn syrup into a small pan, warm over low heat until runny, then add to the bread crumbs and stir well. Beat together the cream and egg and gradually fold them into the syrup mix. Cover the bowl with plastic wrap and refrigerate overnight.

2 Lightly butter a loose-based, fluted 9-in tart pan, roll out the shortcrust pastry until ¼in thick (*see* secret, page 132), and line the pan (*see* secret, page 142). Cover with plastic wrap and refrigerate for at least 20 minutes.

3 Preheat the oven to 300°F.

4 Pour the filling into the pastry pan and bake in the oven for 45–50 minutes, until golden brown and just set.

Making bread crumbs
Simply remove the crusts from day-old bread, roughly chop the bread, throw into the food processor, then process. Seal the crumbs in a plastic food bag and freeze. Add to them whenever you have leftover bread until you have enough to make yourself a treat—like the recipe above—for all your hard work! Bought bread crumbs are relatively expensive and often have artificial ingredients in them that we can all do without.

Pineapple tarte tatin

This has to be one of the prettiest desserts there is, and it looks much more impressive and complicated than it actually is to make! It is especially delicious when served with a scoop of my Coconut sorbet (see page 214). You'll need four 4in tart pans.

Serves 4
Preparation time 10 minutes,
    plus 30 minutes cooking/chilling
Cooking time 20 minutes
Can be made in advance to end of step 3

4¾in thick slices of ripe pineapple
¼ cup superfine sugar
knob of butter (about 2 tbsp)
generous splash of coconut-flavored liqueur
13oz prepared puff pastry sheet

Making caramel

Don't be scared of making caramel, but do take care, as sugar burns are very nasty. Melt the sugar in a clean pan, swirling it occasionally to get an even color (but never stirring). Make sure that every single grain of sugar has melted. Watch it like a hawk as there's a split-second difference between caramel and burned sugar! If it starts to burn, immediately plunge the pan's base into cold water to stop the cooking process.

1 Remove and discard the hard central core from each pineapple slice. Place a skillet over medium heat and add the sugar (see secret, below). Watching constantly, wait until it turns a good caramel color, then add the butter and allow it to melt and bubble. Add a glug of liqueur—watch your eyebrows; it will flame up! Let this mixture bubble together, then divide it between the 4 tart pans and refrigerate it for 10 minutes to cool and firm up.

2 Place a pineapple ring on the top of each caramel base and push it down slightly.

3 Cut out 4 rounds of pastry, each slightly bigger than the tart pans. Drape over the top of the pineapple, then tuck in the edges well to encase the pineapple completely. Refrigerate for up to 20 minutes to prevent the pastry from shrinking in the oven.

4 Preheat the oven to 400°F.

5 Bake for 20–25 minutes, until the tarts are cooked and golden.

6 Remove from the oven and rest for 10 minutes, then very carefully slide a knife around the sides of each tart to loosen. Place a serving plate on top of each, then flip it over to invert the tart tatins. Do this very carefully as caramel can burn!

Fresh cherry jam tart

This is a quick dessert that the kids will love. Replace the cherries with strawberries, raspberries, or blueberries when they're in season if you wish. Just make sure, whichever fruit you use, that it isn't over-ripe, as it needs to hold its shape once cooked.

Serves 4
Preparation time 15 minutes
Cooking time 20 minutes
Can be made in advance to end of step 3

13oz prepared puff pastry sheet,
   cut in half
1lb 2oz fresh cherries, pitted and halved
2 tsp confectioners' sugar
½ cup Pimm's No. 1 liquor
1 tsp cornstarch
1 egg, beaten
1 tbsp light brown sugar

1 Place the pastry squares on a baking sheet lined with parchment paper. Score a square rim 1in from the edge of each (*see secret, below left*) and then refrigerate for 20–30 minutes.

2 Meanwhile, preheat the oven to 400°F and prepare the tart filling. Place a saucepan over medium heat and, when it is hot, toss in the cherries and confectioners' sugar. Stir, then add the Pimm's. Watch out for the flame! Allow the mixture to thicken and bubble.

3 Mix the cornstarch in a small bowl with 2 tsp cold water to make a paste (this is known as slurry) and stir it in with the cherries. When the mixture is syrupy, pour it into a large bowl and allow it to cool completely.

4 Spoon the cherries into the center of each scored square on the pastry, leaving 1in clear around the sides. Brush the pastry rim with egg and sprinkle with the light brown sugar.

5 Cook the tarts in the oven for 15–20 minutes, until the pastry is nicely golden. Allow to cool before serving. Each square will serve 2.

Making a puff pastry rim

It is easy and quick to make sweet or savory tarts with prepared puff pastry, but you will have to create a rim to enclose the filling. To do this, score the pastry (make sure you do not cut all the way through it) with a butter knife. This enables the layers of pastry to puff up while baking. If you neglect to do this, you will have an untidy, perhaps leaking, tart.

Phyllo lemon tart

I particularly like this with lemon marmalade, but of course you can use any flavor of jam you like. Phyllo dough, found in the freezer section of most supermarkets, is lighter than puff pastry, and gives an amazing brittle crust that shatters at the touch of a knife.

Makes 12 slices
Preparation time 15 minutes
Cooking time 20 minutes

8 ready-prepared phyllo dough sheets
 (*see* secret, below)
4 tbsp (½ stick) butter, melted
½ cup lemon marmalade
3 tbsp sunflower seeds
1 tbsp superfine sugar

1 Preheat the oven to 400°F.

2 Find a baking sheet that's about the same size as the phyllo sheets. Brush some butter over the baking sheet, then lay on 4 sheets of phyllo, one by one, buttering between each (*see* secret, below).

3 Place the marmalade in a small bowl and give it a vigorous stir to loosen it up. Spoon it over the phyllo dough, being generous, then sprinkle with half the sunflower seeds. Repeat the layering with the remaining phyllo dough, ending with the top layer buttered, then sprinkle with the remaining sunflower seeds and the sugar.

4 Bake the tart for 20 minutes, until it is golden and crispy at the edges. Remove from the oven, allow to cool for 5 minutes, then cut into slices.

Working with phyllo dough

Phyllo dough is delicious, but quick to dry out. Because of this, you must ensure it is always covered when you work with it; use a clean slightly dampened, clean kitchen towel. Every sheet must be brushed with butter before baking, as otherwise the pastry will be dry and tasteless rather than crispy and delicious. Melt some butter and spread it over the pastry sheet, making sure you cover the entire surface.

Vegetables

Stuffed zucchini · Cauliflower cheese my way · Filled potato skins
Tarka dal · Best-ever homemade fries · Rosemary roasted parsnips
Honey & thyme roasted turnips · Roasted beets with crème fraîche & chives
Green beans with lemon & pancetta · Cream cheese fava beans & peas
Peapod salad · Curly kale with anchovies, onion, & garlic
Pan-fried corn · Stuffed mushrooms · Asparagus soup · Celery soup
Fresh green salad with bacon · Napa cabbage & chile salad
New potato salad with crème fraîche & cilantro

Secrets of cooking vegetables

The most important thing to remember is to shop seasonally and buy locally. Read the labels to see where vegetables are from, and shop by sight and smell. Choose what looks best in the market rather than being led by a recipe. And remember, you can always smell the best tomatoes.

When selecting salad, think what you'll serve it with and go for the colors and textures of leaves that will best complement the rest of your meal. Choose crispy Iceberg lettuce to use as a wrap or to give some crunch with my Filled Potato Skins (*see* page 160), or buy softer Little Gems (baby Romaine) to serve with a shrimp cocktail.

Use your head and save your pennies. There is no need to buy ready-cut vegetables. You will pay a premium and, really, how long will it take to do them yourself? There are other benefits, too: carrots look beautiful when still adorned with their greenery and children love to see them.

Don't attempt to do your vegetable shopping for the whole week in one stop. Of course, you can make sure you have root vegetables in, such as potatoes and carrots, but, if you can, pick up a few fresh, lively greens every couple of days.

Don't just boil vegetables. It may put your children off—mine certainly went through a phase of calling boiled zucchini slimy cucumbers! But once I began to use my imagination and blanched them, then pan-fried them with garlic, lemon zest, and Parmesan until crisp on the outside, they became a favorite.

I am a true believer in steamed vegetables. Gordon thinks it takes too long, but he's wrong! This method retains so much goodness. And you only need one steamer insert on the stovetop, rather than millions of different pans.

When you are faced with a marathon meal to prepare, such as Christmas dinner or a large family gathering, par-boil your vegetables before the chaos begins. That way, you will be ahead of the game as they will need only a brief second cooking before serving.

Never overlook squashes. Butternut squash, especially, is so adaptable. Simply roast it, skin on, with garlic and rosemary, or even dice and mash it. It is the perfect partner to fish or chicken dishes and, when mixed with gravy, it's delicious.

Stuffed zucchini

My mom used to make these, but she stuffed the zucchini with ground meat and grated cheddar cheese over the top. This is great comfort food, and a good way to introduce children to squash. It's also a clever use for late-summer zucchini that have grown fat in the garden. For a larger meal, serve 2 large zucchini rings per person on a bed of rice.

Serves 6 as an appetizer
Preparation time 10 minutes
Cooking time 35 minutes
Can be made in advance to end of step 3

1 large zucchini, trimmed, sliced into
   1in rings and seeded
3 tbsp olive oil
sea salt and black pepper

For the stuffing
1 tbsp olive oil
1 garlic clove, crushed
1 thyme sprig
5 baby zucchini, sliced into ¼in thick disks
8 small plum tomatoes, quartered
⅓ cup bread crumbs
⅓ cup finely grated Parmesan cheese
¼ cup chopped almonds

1 Preheat the oven to 350°F.

2 Place the zucchini rings in an ovenproof dish so they fit snugly. Drizzle with the oil and season with salt and pepper. Cook in the oven for 20 minutes, or until golden and quite soft. Keep the oven on.

3 Meanwhile, make the stuffing. Pour the oil into a pan and place over medium heat. Add the garlic and thyme and fry gently for 1–2 minutes, then add the zucchini disks and stir until they take on a light color. Toss in the tomatoes and sauté for a couple of minutes to break them down a little.

4 Sprinkle half the bread crumbs into the hole in each zucchini ring to soak up any moisture, then divide the stuffing mix between the rings. Sprinkle over the remaining bread crumbs, the Parmesan, and almonds, grind over black pepper and cook in the oven for 15 minutes, or until golden.

Zucchini know-how
Zucchini is an incredibly versatile, wonderfully inexpensive vegetable. But, to make the most of its delicate flavor, avoid steaming or—especially—boiling, as these treatments can lead to something that my children call "slimy cucumbers" on the plate! Instead try baking zucchini, as I do here, or sauté with chopped shallots, garlic, and bacon. This draws out the moisture in the vegetable and renders it firm and delicious.

Cauliflower cheese my way

This is a rich and comforting gratin. I hated bland cauliflower cheese with mushy cauliflower at school—like macaroni cheese with overcooked pasta—but here is a great, light alternative. However, for those who want the more traditional recipe, I have given a method for cheese sauce here as well (see secret, below).

Serves 4 as a side dish
Preparation time 10–15 minutes
Cooking time 25 minutes
Can be made in advance to end of step 3

1 cauliflower
sea salt and black pepper
1 cup plus 2 tbsp crème fraîche
2 egg yolks
½ tbsp finely grated Parmesan cheese
3½oz gorgonzola dolce cheese
3–4 tbsp bread crumbs
pinch of cayenne pepper

1 Preheat the oven to 400°F.

2 Separate the cauliflower into quite large florets. Bring a pan of salted water to a boil over high heat, add the florets and cook for 5–10 minutes until tender (the time it takes will depend on their size). You should be able to pierce a floret without any resistance using a sharp knife. Drain and set aside.

3 Find an ovenproof dish that fits all the florets in snugly, place them in and put in the oven for 5 minutes to dry a little. Remove and drain very well again, then return to the dish.

4 To make the sauce, mix together the crème fraîche, egg yolks, and Parmesan. Season well with pepper and stir. Pour the sauce over the cauliflower, then crumble the gorgonzola over, in large pieces, and sprinkle on the bread crumbs and cayenne pepper.

5 Cook in the oven for 15–20 minutes until golden and bubbling.

How to make a cheese sauce

Traditionally this dish has a cheese sauce and it's useful to know how to make it. Simply melt 3 tbsp butter in a pan over gentle heat and stir in 3 tbsp all-purpose flour. Stir for 3–4 minutes to cook out the raw flour taste, then whisk in 1 cup hot milk, little by little, stirring constantly to avoid lumps. Bubble for 5 minutes, until thickened, then flavor with grated cheese.

Filled potato skins

I love these. The kids first had them in a local restaurant and I've been trying to perfect my version ever since. I see it as a challenge, as children will always tell you the truth when you ask them for their opinion of a dish!

Serves 4
Preparation time 10 minutes
Cooking time 45 minutes
Can be made in advance

4 large baking potatoes, unpeeled
olive oil, to drizzle, plus extra for
    the baking sheet
sea salt and black pepper
4 large eggs
3 tbsp low-fat crème fraîche
½ cup finely chopped watercress
1 tsp cayenne pepper (optional)

1 Preheat the oven to 425°F.

2 Wash and dry the potatoes and prepare and prick the skins (*see* secret, below). Pop them each in a microwave on full power for 13 minutes, or until fully cooked, turning halfway through the cooking time. The potatoes will stay plump instead of shrinking as they can do in the oven.

3 Remove the potatoes, halve lengthwise and remove the soft inner flesh to a bowl, leaving only about ¼in as a shell. Oil a baking sheet, lay on the potato skins, drizzle with more oil, and sprinkle with salt. Bake for 15–20 minutes, until really nice and crispy.

4 Meanwhile, bring a pan of water to the boil and cook the eggs for 5–6 minutes; they should be very slightly soft in the middle. Peel and mash until chunky, then season with salt and pepper. Add the crème fraîche and reserved potato flesh and gently mix through. Reduce the oven temperature to 350°F. Divide the filling between the crispy potato skins and bake for 10 minutes, until piping hot.

5 Remove from the oven and arrange on a serving plate. Sprinkle with the watercress and a little cayenne pepper, if liked.

The best baked potatoes

Choose floury potatoes with a dry texture, such as russets: once baked, they turn beautifully light and fluffy. To make the skins crisp, either wet the potatoes or rub some oil into the skins and roll in sea salt before baking. Always prick the potatoes with a small knife or fork before cooking, especially if you are using a microwave, otherwise you may have a small explosion!

Tarka dal

You will need a saucepan with a tight-fitting lid for this recipe but, in a pinch, use aluminum foil instead. Wrap a double layer tightly around the pot, sealing around the sides so steam can't escape. If the foil is not airtight, the dish will lose moisture and may burn.

Serves 4 as a side dish
Preparation time 10 minutes
Cooking time 30 minutes
Can be made in advance

1 cup split red lentils
2 tsp sea salt
2 tbsp unsalted butter
1 red onion, finely chopped
2 garlic cloves, crushed
1 tsp ground turmeric
2 tsp garam masala
1 tbsp finely chopped cilantro leaves

1 Pour the lentils into a fine-mesh strainer and place under running water to rinse. Transfer them to a saucepan, adding 2 cups cold water, then place over medium heat and bring to a boil. Reduce the heat to a gentle simmer for 10 minutes, skimming any scum off the top, then partly cover with the lid and leave to bubble gently for 20 minutes. You should end up with a hearty yellow soup. Check that the lentils are ready (*see* secret, below), then add the salt.

2 Meanwhile, gently melt the butter in a skillet and add the onion and garlic, stirring for 5–10 minutes, or until they soften. Add the turmeric and garam masala and mix well. Give the lentils a good stir, then add the onion mixture to them and stir through.

3 Season with more salt, if necessary, and stir in the chopped cilantro, reserving 1 tsp to sprinkle over the top when serving.

How to cook lentils

These legumes are a terrific pantry ingredient as they don't need to be soaked before cooking, unlike dried beans and chickpeas. Always rinse lentils before use, as they can be dusty, and place them in a large pan to let them expand as they cook. When ready they should retain their shape but be tender within—taste to check.

Best-ever homemade fries

I love French fries and these are delicious and go with everything. They certainly make a virtuous salad seem like more of a meal! I'm a firm believer in having everything in moderation...but these fries are hard to moderate because they are so good!

Serves 4–6
Preparation time 5 minutes
Cooking time 10 minutes

vegetable oil, for deep-frying
8 russet potatoes, sliced into
   even-sized fries
sea salt

1 Heat the oil in a deep-fryer to 266°F.

2 Place the fries into the fryer and cook for 5 minutes, until slightly softened but without any color. Remove, drain well and blot on paper towels to remove any excess oil, then allow to cool completely.

3 Turn the fryer temperature up to 365°F. Return the fries to the fryer and cook them for 3–4 minutes, or until golden and crispy. Remove from the oil, drain well, and blot again on paper towels. Sprinkle over the salt while the fries are piping hot and serve immediately.

Choosing potatoes for fries

The best fries come from the most suitable potatoes, so select Yukon Gold, russet, or red gold (which have a red skin and yellow flesh) varieties. I use russet here; they have a pleasant floury texture that is ideal not only for French fries but also for roasted potatoes, mashed, and wedges.

Rosemary roasted parsnips

These are especially lovely with roast chicken. The cumin gives them a pungent depth that offsets the sweetness of the parsnips brilliantly, while the rosemary lends them a strong herbal fragrance. Don't be tempted to use more rosemary than suggested here as it can be overpowering.

Serves 4 as a side dish
Preparation time 5 minutes
Cooking time 25–30 minutes

2 tbsp olive oil, plus extra for the pan
6 parsnips (about 1lb 2oz in total),
   halved and cored
12 rosemary sprigs
1 tsp ground cumin
sea salt and black pepper

1 Preheat the oven to 400°F.

2 Line a baking pan that will fit all the parsnips in a single layer with parchment paper, then add in the parsnips, rosemary, oil, and cumin. Season very well with salt and pepper and toss so that all the parsnips are well covered with their seasonings.

3 Cook in the oven for 25–30 minutes, or until the parsnips are slightly golden and crisp, and wonderfully tender within.

Roasting with herbs
Herbs add a wonderful flavor dimension to any roasted dish, whether it's meat, fish, or vegetables. But make sure you use only robust, twiggy herbs for roasting, such as the rosemary here, thyme, or bay leaves; their essential oils will survive the cooking process. Delicate herbs with soft leaves such as parsley, dill, or tarragon will not stand up well to the intense heat, and will simply shrivel and lose their aroma.

Honey & thyme roasted turnips

Turnips are a great-value vegetable. However, they can be bitter, which is often offputting to children. In this recipe, the sweetness of the honey corrects any such tendency. You'll find this makes a popular side dish for everyone at the table.

Serves 4 as a side dish
Preparation time 5–10 minutes
Cooking time 40 minutes
Can be made in advance
Suitable for freezing

1 large turnip (about 1lb 10oz),
    evenly diced
sea salt and black pepper
2 tbsp olive oil
6 thyme sprigs
2 tbsp golden honey
1 tbsp balsamic vinegar

1 Preheat the oven to 350°F.

2 Place the turnip in a pan of cold salted water, bring to a boil over high heat, and cook for 8–10 minutes. Drain well, transfer to a large nonstick roasting pan, and pop into the oven for 5 minutes to dry out. Remove, add the oil and thyme, season with salt and pepper and toss to coat.

3 Drizzle over the honey and balsamic vinegar and roast for 25 minutes, stirring occasionally, until golden and slightly crisp at the edges (*see* secret, below).

Cooking with honey

Nonstick roasting pans and baking sheets are your friends when using honey in the oven. Though it will add a wonderful sweetness and give a beautiful burnished color, it can very easily burn, turning black, acrid in flavor, and impossible to chip off traditional baking ware. Keep a close eye on the dish in the oven, basting and stirring frequently and watching out for any scorching.

Roasted beets with crème fraîche & chives

Delicious, fresh beets are enjoying a revival as people are discovering that there are so many ways to prepare this versatile vegetable—and we're not talking about pickling! One taste of these roasted beets and you'll be a convert!

Serves 4 as a side dish
Preparation time 5 minutes
Cooking time 1 hour

4 fresh beets (each about 4½oz),
   with leaves
4 tbsp olive oil
sea salt and black pepper

To serve
4 tbsp crème fraîche
4 tsp snipped chives

1 Preheat the oven to 375°F.

2 Trim the top leaves, leaving only about 2in attached, then rinse and dry on paper towels. Transfer to a roasting pan (I find it easier to use a loaf pan to contain the beets securely). Drizzle over the oil, season with salt and pepper, and roll the beets around to coat.

3 Roast in the oven for 1 hour, or until a sharp knife easily pierces each beet. Remove from the oven and set aside until cool enough to handle.

4 Wearing clean rubber gloves to prevent staining your hands, slice off the top and the root of each beet, slide off the outer layer of skin, then slice each beet in half vertically—not quite to the bottom— then into quarters, then eighths. Each should open up like a segmented orange. Spoon crème fraîche onto each beet, sprinkle with chives and serve.

Perfect roasted vegetables

Cut all your vegetables into similar-size pieces for even cooking. The smaller the pieces, the quicker the roasting time. However, be prepared for hard root vegetables, such as potatoes and carrots, to take up to 1 hour, while soft vegetables, such as bell peppers or eggplants, should need just 20–30 minutes. Toss or drizzle the vegetables with plain olive oil (keep the expensive extra-virgin variety for dressings) and make sure they are evenly coated, then season with salt and pepper. You can choose to add whole garlic cloves and robust herbs such as thyme or rosemary at this stage, if you like. Toss the vegetables once or twice during cooking so they roast evenly. They are done when tender (test with a small, sharp knife) and beginning to crisp at the edges.

Green beans with lemon & pancetta

It's not easy to get children to eat vegetables, but sweet green beans are a good place to start. The lemon here gives them a great zing, while the pancetta helps ensure they disappear in no time. As with all vegetables, never overcook green beans or they will be bitter and dull.

Serves 4 as a side dish
Preparation time 5 minutes
Cooking time 10 minutes

½lb green beans, trimmed and halved
2¾oz pancetta, or bacon, cubed
2 tbsp pine nuts
finely grated zest of 1 lemon (about 3 tsp)
sea salt and black pepper

1 Blanch the beans for a couple of minutes, then shock in cold water (*see* secret, below), making sure they don't remain too firm or they will squeak when eaten.

2 Place a nonstick skillet over medium heat and fry the pancetta, stirring occasionally, until it has released its fat and is crispy and golden. Add the pine nuts and toss for 1–2 minutes more until they take on a toasted color. Add the drained beans and heat through, mixing everything together. Finally, add the lemon zest, season to taste with salt and pepper and serve.

Blanching vegetables

The term "blanch" refers to quick cooking in boiling water. Bring a large pan of salted water to a boil over high heat, then add the cleaned and trimmed vegetables. Boil for the time specified in the recipe, drain well and plunge into ice-cold water. This is called "shocking" the vegetables. Blanching helps to set the color so, whether you choose to cook the vegetables further or not, they will always remain brightly colored.

Cream cheese fava beans & peas

I use a light cream cheese for this recipe, but you should choose the type you like best. This is a great way of disguising healthy greens to make them more appealing to children, and is delicious with my Ricotta, Pepper, & Artichoke Quiche (see page 130).

Serves 4 as a side dish
Preparation time 5 minutes,
   plus 30 minutes podding
Cooking time 5–10 minutes
Can be made in advance
Suitable for freezing

1 cup fava beans (shelled weight)
1 cup peas (shelled weight)
1 tbsp olive oil
3–4 tbsp light cream cheese
1½ tbsp finely grated Parmesan cheese
small handful of flatleaf parsley, chopped
sea salt and black pepper

1 Blanch the fava beans for 2 minutes, shock in ice-cold water (*see* secret, page 170), then remove the skin from each bean (*see* secret, below). If using fresh peas, blanch for 1 minute, then shock them also.

2 Pour the olive oil into a pan over medium-low heat, add the peas and fava beans and stir. Spoon in the cream cheese and sprinkle over the Parmesan, stirring to coat the beans and peas. Add the parsley and gently simmer for no more than a couple of minutes, adding a splash of water if needed to stop the mixture from drying out. Season to taste with salt and pepper and serve immediately.

Double-shelling fava beans

Toward the end of the season, when these beans are older and larger, they may need double-shelling. This process gives an extra-tender fava bean. You need a little time and patience to do this, but it can be a relaxing process. Blanch the fava beans (*see* secret, page 170), then peel each one by squeezing it between your fingers. The outer skin will slip off to reveal the bright green bean beneath. Discard the outer skin.

Peapod salad

Peapods are an incredibly versatile vegetable. They are wonderful in salads and stir-fries, and can also serve as the "greens" to go with any main meal. This dish tastes great with lots of different recipes, but it's especially good with Asian-influenced flavors.

Serves 4 as a side dish
Preparation time 5 minutes
Cooking time 5 minutes

1 cup peapods, trimmed
1 tbsp olive oil
½ cup fresh bean sprouts
sea salt and black pepper
1 tbsp soy sauce

1 Blanch the peapods for 2 minutes, then shock in ice-cold water (*see* secret, page 170).

2 Pour the oil into a pan over medium heat, toss in the peapods and stir to heat through. Add the bean sprouts and heat through for a couple more minutes, stirring, then season with salt and pepper, going easy on the salt as you will be adding soy sauce.

3 Drizzle with the soy sauce, then serve immediately.

Bean sprouts

In this recipe, the bean sprouts complement the peapods perfectly, as both have a crisp bite that makes the salad very easy to eat. Available in bags in most supermarkets, bean sprouts can be used to add bulk and bite to stir-fries with noodles. They are highly nutritious, but if you eat them raw—as some seem to encourage—you miss out on their protein, which is released through cooking.

Curly kale with anchovies, onion, & garlic

This dish would work equally well with savoy cabbage or baby bok choy, but, if you're using young, sweet spring greens, you won't need to cook them any further after you add them back to the pan. Instead, simply warm them through with the other ingredients.

Serves 4 as a side dish
Preparation time 5–10 minutes
Cooking time 15 minutes

3 cups curly kale, trimmed (*see* secret, below)
2 tbsp olive oil
2 garlic cloves, finely sliced
1 large onion, finely sliced
3 tbsp red wine vinegar
3 canned anchovies, drained and
    finely chopped
sea salt and black pepper

1 Blanch the kale for 1–2 minutes, then shock in ice-cold water (*see* secret, page 170), and shake thoroughly to dry.

2 Pour the oil into a pan over low heat and add the garlic and onion. Cook, stirring, for 2–3 minutes until softened. Add the vinegar and the anchovies and continue to fry for 2–3 minutes, then return the kale. Pour in ¼–½ cup of water to help steam the kale, and season well with salt and pepper. Cook for 5–6 minutes, stirring, then serve immediately.

Tackling curly kale

Kale can be a baffling vegetable to prepare if you're unfamiliar with it, but it has a delicious strong taste and is very good for you. Choose a bright green bunch, wash it well, and tear the frilly leaves from their tough central stalks. Larger leaves can be sliced or shredded if you want. This recipe is great, but try kale in a stir-fry or sauté as well. Bacon makes a wonderful addition.

Pan-fried corn

As a family we love corn on the cob. Megan, our eldest daughter, now has braces and really misses it—so I invented these smaller versions that she can still manage. You can choose to barbecue this recipe if you prefer (see secret, below).

Serves 4 as a side dish
Preparation time 5 minutes
Cooking time 20 minutes

4 ears of corn
sea salt and black pepper
2 tbsp olive oil
4 tbsp (½ stick) unsalted butter
½ tbsp fresh rosemary, finely chopped

1 Place the corn into a pan of boiling salted water, bring back to a boil, and simmer for 10 minutes (you can't really overcook them).

2 When the kernels are tender to the tip of a knife, drain them and set aside until cool enough to handle. Using a very sharp knife, slice each ear into rings of about 1in thick and season with salt and pepper.

3 Heat the oil in a skillet and add the corn, in batches if necessary. Fry, turning, until the corn is golden on all sides. Add the butter and rosemary and spoon it over the rings (be careful of any spitting butter). Allow the corn to become a nice nutty golden color.

4 Transfer the corn to a plate, pouring over the remaining butter and rosemary. Sprinkle over a little more salt and leave until cool enough to pick up and eat. Serve warm.

Sweet corn on the barbecue

If you'd like to try this recipe on the barbecue, simply follow the recipe to the end of step 2, then toss the rings in the oil. Wrap them in foil to protect them from direct flames, and place the packet on the barbecue for 5–10 minutes, turning once. The sweet corn will pick up a lovely smoky flavor. Remove from the heat, then spoon the butter and rosemary into the packet.

Stuffed mushrooms

This is great as an appetizer or side dish. The quantities are substantial, and it's excellent for vegetarians if you leave out the pancetta. Cooking the large white mushrooms in the oven rather than in a skillet means they retain all their juices.

Serves 4
Preparation time 15 minutes
Cooking time 35 minutes
Can be made in advance

8 large mushrooms, stems removed and
   finely chopped
2 tbsp butter, cut into 8 cubes
1 garlic clove, finely chopped
1 tbsp finely chopped parsley
1 red onion, finely chopped
2¾oz pancetta, or bacon, cubed
1 bay leaf
½ cup white wine
2 tbsp crème fraîche
3 tbsp bread crumbs (*see* secret, page 143)

1 Preheat the oven to 400°F.

2 Clean the mushrooms (*see* secret, below). Place them, gills up, in an ovenproof dish and drop a cube of butter onto each. Bake for 20 minutes.

3 Meanwhile, in a small bowl, mix together the chopped mushroom stems, garlic, parsley, and onion. Fry the pancetta in a dry skillet until it renders its fat, then add the mushroom stem mix and allow it to soften for a minute. Throw in the bay leaf, then add the wine and leave to bubble and reduce for a couple of minutes. Turn the heat down, then stir through the crème fraîche. Take the pan off the heat and fish out the bay leaf.

4 Divide this stuffing between the mushrooms, then sprinkle over the bread crumbs to add texture and color. Return the mushrooms to the oven for 15 minutes more, until golden brown.

How to clean mushrooms

Never rinse mushrooms with water or—worse still—plunge them into it, as they are like sponges and will soak the liquid up, rendering them tasteless and hard to cook successfully. Instead, wipe them either with a damp paper towel or a soft brush reserved for the purpose, to remove any grit and soil. Many kitchen supply stores sell mushroom brushes expressly for this.

Asparagus soup

White or green asparagus can be used here, but green doesn't look as posh as white! To add texture to this dish, cut off the asparagus tips, make the soup as directed, then boil the tips in water for a minute, drain, chop into ¼in lengths and place them in the bottom of the serving bowls, before pouring the soup on top.

Serves 6 as an appetizer
Preparation time 10 minutes
Cooking time 10–15 minutes
Can be made in advance to end of step 2
Suitable for freezing at end of step 2

1lb 10oz white (or green) asparagus, trimmed (*see* secret, below)
2 tbsp unsalted butter
2 shallots, finely sliced
3½ cups good-quality, hot chicken stock (*see* secret, page 37)
2 tbsp crème fraîche
sea salt and black pepper

To serve
toasted crusty white bread
few drops of truffle oil

1 Chop the asparagus into 1in pieces. Melt the butter in a large saucepan over low heat and gently sauté the shallots for 2–3 minutes, or until softened but not colored. Add the asparagus and cook, stirring, for 5–10 minutes, or until it begins to soften. Add the hot chicken stock and remove from the heat.

2 Pour the soup into a blender and process until smooth. You may have to do this in batches as the blender should be no more than half full each time to avoid splashing; hold the lid on with a kitchen towel to protect your hands from the hot liquid.

3 Return the soup to the pan to warm through gently, stir in the crème fraîche and season with salt and pepper to taste. Serve in warmed bowls, accompanied by buttered toast, topping with a drizzle of truffle oil and another pinch of pepper.

Choosing and preparing asparagus
You can find white asparagus in specialty markets. It is white because it is grown under the soil and is slightly more tender and delicate in flavor than green asparagus. To trim asparagus spears, snap off and remove the woody stalk at the bottom; handily, it will break at the right place. You can discard these pieces or use as part of a vegetable stock. Thicker spears will need to be peeled of the tougher skin toward the base.

Celery soup

Soups are immensely comforting, but can also be impressive at a dinner party (with the added bonus that you can make them in advance). For variety, try adding ½–1 teaspoon curry powder as you cook down the celery, or crumble a little Stilton over the top.

Serves 6
Preparation time 5–10 minutes
Cooking time 45–50 minutes
Can be made in advance to end of step 2
Suitable for freezing at end of step 2

7 tbsp butter
2 bunches of celery, trimmed, cut into
    1in pieces
5 cups chicken stock (*see* secret, page 37)
¾ cup walnuts
½ cup heavy cream

1 Gently melt the butter in a large saucepan, then add the celery and its leaves. Allow to bubble, stirring occasionally, for 15–20 minutes, or until the celery is completely soft (*see* secret, below). Add the chicken stock and bring to a boil. Reduce the heat once more and simmer for another 15–20 minutes.

2 Add the walnuts and cook for 4–5 minutes, then transfer the soup to a blender and process until smooth. You may have to do this in batches as the blender should be no more than half full each time to avoid splashing; hold the lid on with a kitchen towel to protect your hands from the hot liquid.

3 Stir in the heavy cream and return the soup to a clean pan over medium heat until piping hot. Serve immediately.

The secret of perfect soup

With this or any other soup, there is an easy—though often overlooked—way to make the flavors sing. The key is patience. When starting a soup base, either with the celery in this recipe or more usually with onions, carrots, and other aromatic roots, cook them gently in butter for a long time (about 20 minutes) to intensify their tastes. Stir occasionally to prevent sticking.

Fresh green salad with bacon

This salad is simple, highly nutritious, and very good to eat. Top with a poached egg to be extra fancy, or serve it with my Best-ever Homemade Fries (see page 164) on the side if it seems too healthy for you or you need a more substantial meal.

Serves 4 as a main course
Preparation time 15 minutes
Cooking time 10 minutes
Can be made in advance to end of step 3

1 cup peas (shelled weight)
1 cup fava beans (podded weight)
6 slices of smoked bacon
4 handfuls of arugula
4 handfuls of baby spinach
2 endive heads, leaves separated
3 tbsp creamy mustard vinaigrette
   (*see* page 276)

How to make and dress a salad

Make sure all the leaves are very well washed and then meticulously dried. Damp leaves will never be crisp. Always apply the dressing at the last minute. This will ensure the leaves remain fresh and vibrant—adding the dressing too early will turn the salad limp and soggy. The dressing can be made in a clean jam jar. Place all the ingredients into the jar and, with the lid securely on, shake vigorously to combine. Any leftover dressing can be stored in the refrigerator.

1 Bring to a boil over high heat a large pan of water that fits your steamer. Place the peas and fava beans in the steamer over the boiling water. Cover and cook for 3 minutes. Meanwhile, fill a large bowl with ice and water. Drain the cooked peas and beans, then plunge them immediately into the ice water to refresh (*see* secret, page 170). Drain again, and transfer them onto paper towels to dry.

2 Place a skillet over high heat. When it is hot, fry the bacon until crispy, then blot on paper towels to remove any excess fat. Allow to cool, then cut into strips.

3 Wash and dry the leaves, and place them in a large salad bowl with the peas, beans, and bacon. If preparing in advance, cover with plastic wrap and leave in the refrigerator for up to 2 hours. Remove from the refrigerator ahead of serving; nothing is more tasteless than "fridge-cold" salad.

4 Just before serving, give the vinaigrette a good whisk and pour it over the salad, tossing well so all the ingredients are coated.

Napa cabbage & chile salad

This fresh, clean-tasting, warm salad is great served alongside a rich and substantial meat dish; try it with my Marinated Duck Breasts (see page 63) for a delicious combination of flavors and textures. Be careful with the toasted sesame oil: it's strong and can be overpowering.

Serves 4 as a side dish
Preparation time 5–10 minutes
Cooking time 5 minutes

1 head of napa cabbage, stem removed,
 thinly shredded
1 red chile, seeds left in, finely sliced
 (*see* secret, below)
3 scallions, sliced at an angle into ¼in pieces
1 tbsp toasted sesame oil
1 tbsp soy sauce
2 tbsp sesame seeds, toasted
sea salt and black pepper

1 Place the napa cabbage, chile, and scallions in a large mixing bowl. Add the oil, soy sauce, and sesame seeds and carefully mix everything together.

2 Place a deep skillet over medium heat. Add the salad along with 2 tbsp water to help steam the vegetables. Cook, stirring occasionally, for no more than 3 minutes, to retain a good crunch to the leaf. Season to taste with salt and pepper and serve straight from the pan.

Chile know-how
Generally speaking, the smaller the chile, the hotter it is. As you prepare chiles, your skin will absorb their capsaicin, which gives a burning, throbbing sensation. Touching a chile and then rubbing your eyes is not a pleasant experience, so be careful! To reduce the heat of any dish, remove chile seeds and membrane with a teaspoon, as this is where the spicy chemical is found.

New potato salad
with crème fraîche & cilantro

This is a classic and a dish you can keep in the refrigerator to use in children's lunchboxes or a Saturday family meal of leftovers. It's a very adaptable recipe as well; try adding bits of crispy bacon or your favorite herbs to jazz it up.

Serves 4
Preparation time 10 minutes
Cooking time 20–25 minutes
Can be made in advance

1lb 2oz Yukon Gold new potatoes,
    larger ones halved (*see* secret, below)
sea salt and black pepper
1 tbsp olive oil
3 tbsp crème fraîche
4 scallions, finely chopped
1 tbsp red wine vinegar
small handful of finely chopped cilantro

1 Place the potatoes in a pan and cover with cold water, adding a pinch of salt. Bring to a boil and simmer for 20–25 minutes, until just tender to the tip of a knife.

2 Drain the potatoes and transfer into a mixing bowl. Drizzle over the oil and allow to cool for 10 minutes.

3 In a separate bowl, mix together the crème fraîche, scallions, and vinegar. Spoon this mixture into the bowl with the potatoes and gently toss, ensuring they are all covered. Season with salt and pepper, then fold in the cilantro. Serve at room temperature.

The best potatoes for salad

You will need waxy potatoes for salad, such as the Yukon Golds I use in this recipe, or you could try red potatoes or the fingerling varieties that are increasingly easy to find. These are firm enough not to break up in the dressing, especially if you take care to cook them only until just tender. Peel them after cooking if you wish, when their skins slip off easily, and dress while still warm so they absorb all the flavors.

A bit of dough

Easy handmade white bread · Pizza dough · Perfect pizza

Tomato & prosciutto bruschetta · Scones for the perfect afternoon tea

Secrets of preparing dough

Many people are scared of making bread. I started when I was training for a marathon with my good friend Jo. While running, we had long conversations about food. She swore by the bread machine that she uses religiously every day. I loved the thought of homemade bread, so I researched recipes I could make, simply, without a machine. Finally I came up with my Easy Handmade White Bread (*see* page 194) and I've used the recipe ever since. It's so much lighter than most loaves. And I was inspired by Jo's bread talk!

We have a rule in our house: if we buy sliced bread, we only ever get whole grain. I never buy sliced white bread, but I always have an emergency loaf in the freezer.

When you make your own bread, you'll know exactly what's in it. Use a variety of seeds, such as pumpkin or sesame, or even add walnuts or raisins for a loaf that is wonderful with blue cheese.

You'll never regret learning to make pizza dough (*see* page 196). Children always love to eat whatever they have made themselves, and this is the perfect way to let them make their own dinner. Rustle up a batch of dough in the morning, wrap it in plastic wrap, and keep it in the refrigerator. It's so much easier than you might think.

Have a children's pizza party with my Perfect Pizza (*see* page 198). In our house, the rule is that the kids always have to have three "nice" things (which means vegetables) before they indulge themselves with the less wholesome toppings! For adults, throw on a handful of arugula when the pizza comes out of the oven.

Knowing how to make bruschetta (*see* page 200) will get you out of all sorts of fixes. Kids love it, and you can easily tweak the recipe to serve as a canapé at most adult gatherings. Try adding red wine to the tomatoes for a sophisticated twist, or add chopped chicken, cilantro, chile, and mango for an exotic bite.

Make my Scones for the Perfect Afternoon Tea (*see* page 202) for the children to eat when you have only half an hour between the end of school and the start of their swimming lessons. It's a nice way to tide them over until supper time.

Easy handmade white bread

I own a bread machine, but in all honesty it sits gathering dust and is pulled out only when I feel guilty for not using it! The only way I really enjoy making bread is by hand and in the simplest way possible. This recipe is so easy and quick, and the bread is really light.

Makes 2 (1lb) loaves
Preparation time 10–15 minutes,
   plus 1½–2 hours rising
Cooking time 40–45 minutes
Can be made in advance
Suitable for freezing

5 cups bread flour, plus extra to dust
2 × ¼oz envelopes instant dry yeast
2 tbsp brown sugar
1 tbsp salt
sunflower oil, for the bowl

1 In a large bowl, mix together the flour, yeast, sugar, and salt. Stir in 2¼ cups of tepid water and mix into a soft dough. Using an electric stand mixer fitted with a dough hook, knead the dough for 5 minutes, or turn it onto a floured surface and knead well by hand for 10–15 minutes.

2 Place the dough in a large oiled bowl and cover with a damp, clean kitchen towel or plastic wrap. Leave in a warm place to rise for 1½–2 hours until doubled in size.

3 Punch down the dough, briefly knead again, then divide into 2 pieces. Shape each into a round loaf or other shape (*see* secret, below) and place on a floured baking sheet. Unless you are making a braid, score a cross in the top of each loaf with a sharp knife.

4 Place the bread in the middle of a cold oven and slide a pan of hot water into the bottom of the oven to create steam, which forms a good crust. Turn the oven to 350°F and bake for 35 minutes, until golden. When the loaves are done (*see* secret, below), transfer to a wire rack to cool.

Shaping dough

Try making other shapes from dough. For a braid, split the dough into 3 equal-size parts and roll each into a thin log. Pinch the ends together and braid the dough, tucking the other ends underneath. Alternatively, knot logs of dough, or form them into breadsticks. Make smaller balls for rolls, dusting with flour before baking. Smaller loaves need shorter cooking times. To test if bread is cooked, tap on the bottom: a cooked loaf rings hollow.

Pizza dough

This is a simple recipe, so don't be afraid to tackle it. You can keep all the ingredients in your pantry and throw the dough together on very short notice for any occasion. Make it in the morning, then refrigerate for an afternoon children's pizza party.

Makes enough for 4 large pizzas
Preparation time 25 minutes,
    plus 1–2 hours rising
Can be made in advance

1 × ¼oz envelope active dry yeast
2 tsp golden honey
2 tbsp extra virgin olive oil,
    plus extra for the bowl
4 cups bread flour, plus extra to dust
1 tsp salt
1 tsp ground black pepper

1 Pour ½ cup warm water into a bowl and stir in the yeast to dissolve. Leave in a warm place for 10 minutes. Add the honey and oil to the yeast and combine well.

2 Sift the flour, salt, and pepper into a large mixing bowl. Make a well in the center and pour in the yeast mixture, mixing until you have a soft, slightly sticky dough. Gradually add more warm water if needed, to achieve the right consistency.

3 Tip the dough onto a lightly floured surface and lightly flour your hands. Knead for 10 minutes, or until the dough is elastic and easy to handle.

4 Lightly oil a large mixing bowl that is big enough to allow the dough to rise. Put in the dough and cover with a damp, clean kitchen towel or plastic wrap. Leave in a warm place for 1–2 hours, until doubled in size.

5 Take out the dough and punch it down until smooth, kneading. Divide into 4 balls and leave, wrapped in plastic wrap, in the refrigerator, until ready to use.

Bread and warmth
Whether making pizza or bread dough, you must always use warm water. If it is too cold, the yeast will not activate; if too hot, you risk killing the yeast. Leave the dough to rise in a warm place to enable the yeast to continue making the bubbles in the dough that will give a light, airy result. A warm kitchen counter is perfect.

Perfect pizza

I love pizza topped with the ingredients I describe here. But a pizza is a very personal thing, and is a great blank canvas. For an unusual topping that's a winner with everyone—especially children—try poaching chicken, cutting it into slices, then drizzling over some barbecue sauce.

Serves 1
Preparation time 10 minutes
Cooking time 10–15 minutes
Can be made in advance

1 ball of Pizza Dough (*see* page 196)
flour, to dust
6 tbsp Tomato Sauce (*see* page 278)
6 slices salami
12 canned anchovies in oil, drained
6 basil leaves, roughly chopped
2 tbsp finely grated Parmesan cheese

1 Preheat the oven to 450°F, placing a heavy-duty baking sheet inside.

2 Place the dough ball on a lightly floured work surface and form your pizza base (*see* secret, below). You want to end up with a base approximately ¼in thick.

3 Lay the pizza base on a piece of parchment paper. Spoon on the tomato sauce, smoothing it right up to the edges. Arrange the salami over the pizza, followed by the anchovies and basil. Finish it off by sprinkling over the Parmesan.

4 Slide the pizza onto the hot baking sheet inside the oven and bake for 10–15 minutes, until crisp and golden.

Shaping pizza bases

Push your ball of dough flat, then pick it up and slap it onto a floured work surface a couple of times. Then either drape it over a clenched fist and stretch gently from the outside rim (you could even twirl it like the professionals do!) or just roll out with a rolling pin. If you prefer a slightly thicker base, reduce the oven temperature so the pizza cooks all the way through without burning on top.

Tomato & prosciutto bruschetta

These make a great appetizer, snack, or light lunch, or even canapés for a cocktail party (make them smaller and neater for that, though). Depending on the occasion and your palate, try topping with tomato, basil, mozzarella, anchovies, or olives. The only limit is your imagination!

Serves 4 as an appetizer
Preparation time 5 minutes
Cooking time 15 minutes
Can be made in advance to end of step 2

1 tbsp olive oil, plus extra to drizzle
7oz small plum tomatoes, sliced lengthwise
½ tbsp oregano leaves
1 tbsp balsamic vinegar
sea salt and black pepper
6 slices prosciutto
1 ciabatta loaf
1 garlic clove, halved
¼ cup finely grated Parmesan cheese

Toast—nature's own grater!

It is astonishing how effectively a toasted slice of bread acts as a grater for garlic. Halve a garlic clove and rub the cut surface over the toast. The clove will begin to disappear as you do so, transferring all its aromatic pulp and juices to the bread. Try this before serving up mushrooms on toast and you'll never look back.

1 Heat the oil in a skillet and toss in the tomatoes to warm through and break down slightly. Add the oregano, balsamic vinegar, and black pepper. Stir to combine, remove from the heat and allow to cool slightly.

2 Fry the prosciutto in a dry nonstick pan over a high heat until crispy and golden, then place on paper towels to blot off the excess oil.

3 Preheat the broiler to its highest setting. Cut the ciabatta in half lengthwise, then slice each half into 2 equal portions.

4 Drizzle olive oil over the cut side of each piece of ciabatta. Sprinkle over a little salt and place under the broiler until golden brown. Rub with the garlic (*see* secret, below).

5 Crumble the prosciutto over the ciabatta slices, then spoon on the tomato mixture and sprinkle with the Parmesan and some more black pepper. Serve hot.

Scones for the perfect afternoon tea

These are perfect served slightly warm with clotted cream and jam. They do keep until the next day, but are best with the scent of the oven still dancing around them. Try to make them when you know the batch will be devoured in a single sitting—preferably not by you on your own!

Makes 9 scones
Preparation time 10–15 minutes
Cooking time 10–12 minutes
Can be made in advance
Suitable for freezing

2 cups all-purpose flour, plus extra to dust
good pinch of salt
2 tsp baking powder
8 tbsp (1 stick) butter
⅓ cup raisins
1 egg
½ cup milk

To serve
strawberry jam
whipping cream

1 Preheat the oven to 400°F.

2 Sift the flour with the salt and baking powder into a large bowl. Cut in the butter in knobs, then rub it into the flour with your fingertips until the mixture resembles bread crumbs. Stir in the raisins.

3 Beat together the egg and milk, add to the flour mixture and stir through until it forms a dough. Knead lightly on a floured surface, then roll or pat the dough flat and, using a 2in fluted round cutter, cut out your scones (*see* secret, below).

4 Place the scones on a baking sheet lined with parchment paper and bake for 10–12 minutes or until lightly golden. Leave to cool slightly, then serve as soon as possible.

5 Serve each scone cut in half and topped with spoonfuls of strawberry jam and whipping cream.

Perfect scones

Handle the dough gently, work quickly, and do not over-knead or the scones will be chewy and tough. Don't roll (or pat out) the dough any thinner than ¾in or you will end up with cookies. Flour the cutter before you cut out the scones; this will prevent the dough from sticking to it and help the scones to rise more evenly.

Something sweet

Meringues · Eton mess · Blackberry ice cream · Coconut sorbet
Orange sorbet · Raspberry sorbet · Melon cooler · Frozen fruit
Pineapple with a lime twist · Mango & passion fruit dessert
Caramelized peaches with hazelnut crème fraîche
Apricot, raspberry, & ginger crumble · Plum & almond pudding
Pear & ginger steamed sponge pudding · Homemade ginger lemonade
Cherry & chocolate mousse · Chocolate cheesecake
Simple Champagne cocktail

Secrets of making desserts

As a family we eat a lot of fruit, especially during summer when I don't want fatty food. On a sunny day, when the children are playing in the wading pool and Gordon and I are drinking a glass of wine in the garden, we all want something light to snack on. So I prepare a platter of fruit and a bowl of strawberries with chopped mint and a sprinkling of balsamic vinegar, which makes a fantastic combination. Try it!

Though I love desserts, we don't have them from Monday to Friday. They are a weekend treat. Since I've taken up running, I don't have to worry about eating them. These days I run farther and eat more!

When I go shopping with the children they are always drawn to the beautiful, intriguing pineapples and they want me to buy them. So I developed my Pineapple with a Lime Twist (*see* page 222). It's something nice to do with a pineapple that doesn't involve skewering chunks on toothpicks! It feels exotic and is very welcome on a summer day.

The only fruit I have all year round—because I've heard they are great brain food—is blueberries. They are a pick-me-up, giving a little sunshine on those dull days.

Frozen Fruit (*see* page 221) is my new craze. I started making it after a friend instructed me to try freezing red grapes. They were a revelation—when you bite into them it's like a lovely sorbet in the center. They are so nice to serve after a meal, while you are finishing your wine. Remove from the refrigerator 10 minutes before serving to take the frozen edge off and present them in little bowls. The kids adore them, too.

Sorbets and ice creams are not an everyday treat but if we have people coming to dinner I make double so we have some left in the freezer for the family. I don't have an ice cream machine; you don't need one either.

Crumbles (*see* page 226) are my favorite dessert. When making them, concentrate on using good-quality fruit and simply prepare it in the old-fashioned way. Never over-complicate it. A spoonful of crumble in a bowl rather than something restauranty that's been meticulously tweaked is my idea of dessert heaven.

Meringues

The secret to perfect meringue is to bake it as slowly as possible on a low heat. My mom used to leave them in the coolest oven of her Aga to cook overnight. Remember that you are not baking them so much as drying them out.

Makes 20 meringues of 2in diameter
Preparation time 30 minutes
Cooking time 5 hours
Can be made in advance
Suitable for freezing for up to 1 month

4 egg whites
1 tbsp lemon juice
1¼ cups superfine sugar

Perfect meringues

Use an immaculately clean glass, china, or stainless-steel bowl when making meringues; avoid plastic, as it may retain grease that will make it hard to whip the egg whites. Make sure you do not have any yolk in the egg white as, again, the fat will prevent it from beating properly. Use eggs at room temperature (older eggs are best, rather than fresh) as they beat better than cold eggs. The meringue has been whipped enough when you can hold the bowl upside down without it falling out! Bake meringues at a low temperature to stop them from browning and cool them slowly in the oven to minimize cracking. Keep in an airtight container for up to a week.

1 Preheat the oven to 200°F.

2 Place the egg whites in a clean glass or stainless-steel mixing bowl, ensuring all your utensils are spotless and dry. If you have a hand-held electric mixer, use it, otherwise you are going to need a handheld whisk and very strong arms! Beat the egg whites until they are foamy, then increase the speed, add the lemon juice, and beat until the mixture is stiff enough to form peaks when the beaters are removed. Add the sugar and mix to combine. The mixture should be glossy.

3 Line a baking sheet with parchment paper. Spoon small 1 tbsp portions of the meringue onto the baking sheet, using a whipping action with the spoon each time to form a peak on top of each. The meringues should be about 2in in diameter.

4 Transfer the meringues to the oven and bake for 5 hours. They are ready when they can be lifted easily off the parchment paper and sound hollow when tapped gently underneath. Turn off the oven and leave the meringues inside until they have cooled completely.

Eton mess

This is one of my favorite desserts. The recipe is inspired by the strawberry, meringue, and cream dessert traditionally served at the British boarding school Eton College on the day of their annual cricket game against students of Winchester College. I adore the different textures: the brittle, dry meringue surrounded by creaminess and fruit. I'd even go as far as to say it's better than chocolate! For extra crunch, sprinkle the top with chopped pistachios or hazelnuts.

Serves 6
Preparation time 15 minutes
Can be made in advance

2 pints strawberries, hulled
1 tbsp confectioners' sugar
2 cups heavy cream
½ recipe meringues (*see* page 208)

1 Cut all the strawberries in half, then put half of them into a blender with the confectioners' sugar. Process until smooth and set aside (*see* secret, below).

2 In a large mixing bowl, whip the cream until thickened, but not stiff. Fold in the remaining strawberries. Carefully break the meringues into pieces and fold them into the strawberry-cream mixture until evenly blended.

3 Drizzle most of the strawberry puree into the mixture, folding just until streaked throughout with the puree. Serve in dessert glasses or bowls drizzled with the reserved strawberry puree.

Beautifying Eton mess

Be careful to fold in the strawberry puree slowly and don't over-work the mixture as you want to create a striking "ripple" effect. For a smoother finish, pour the strawberry puree through a fine-mesh strainer to remove any seeds.

Blackberry ice cream

This is heaven. You can't easily find this flavor in the shops, and it's one that takes me back to my childhood. I would often go blackberrying and, in the autumn, would collect an abundance of the fruits. The kids love this ice cream, too, especially as it stains their tongues purple!

Makes about 1¾ pints
Preparation time 30 minutes,
   plus overnight freezing
Cooking time 10–12 minutes
Can be made in advance

2 pints blackberries
2 tbsp golden honey
⅓ cup superfine sugar
13.4oz can evaporated milk
½ cup plus 2 tbsp heavy cream, whipped
3 tbsp lemon juice

1 Place the blackberries, honey, and sugar into a medium saucepan. Cook gently over low heat for 10–12 minutes, or until the blackberries are soft and slightly mushy. Transfer the mixture to a blender and process until smooth. Pass through a fine-mesh strainer into a clean bowl and allow to cool.

2 Meanwhile, in another large bowl, whip the evaporated milk until slightly thickened. Fold in the cream, blackberry puree, and lemon juice.

3 Pour the mixture into a lidded plastic container and place in the freezer for 45 minutes, or until it is beginning to freeze around the edges. Remove, pour into a chilled bowl (or the bowl of a food processor), and beat until smooth and creamy. Repeat this freezing and beating process twice more (*see* secret, below), then return to the freezer until ready to serve. If using an ice-cream machine, churn for 1 hour instead, then turn into a lidded plastic container and store in the freezer.

Making ice creams and sorbets without an ice cream machine

If you don't have an ice cream machine you can still make wonderful sorbets and ice creams, but you must beat the mixture—by hand or in a food processor—3 times during the freezing process. This avoids the formation of ice crystals and creates a smoother result. Place the sorbet or ice cream container (such as a plastic tub) in the freezer before you add the mixture, as it will help speed up the process, and do the same with the bowl in which you intend to beat the mixture.

Coconut sorbet

This is wonderful served alongside my Pineapple Tart Tatin (see page 145). It is something a bit different and reminds me of summer, especially with a bit of coconut liqueur poured over the top. I'm a huge sorbet fan; they are light and delicious and an excellent way to satisfy sweet cravings.

Makes about 1¾ pints
Preparation time 30 minutes,
    plus overnight freezing
Cooking time 5 minutes
Can be made in advance

1¾ cups superfine sugar
13.5oz can coconut milk
1 tsp glycerin

1 Put the sugar into a pan with 1¾ cups cold water. Place over medium heat until all the sugar has dissolved, then set aside for 30 minutes to cool.

2 Whisk the coconut milk to remove any lumps, then pour it into the cooled sugar syrup along with the glycerin.

3 Pour the mixture into a lidded plastic container and place in the freezer for 45 minutes, or until it is beginning to freeze around the edges. Remove, tip into a chilled bowl (or the bowl of a food processor), and beat until smooth and creamy. Repeat this freezing and beating process twice more (*see* secret, page 212), then return to the freezer until ready to serve. If using an ice-cream machine, churn for 1 hour instead, then turn into a lidded plastic container and store in the freezer.

4 Remove from the freezer at least 10 minutes before serving to soften slightly, for maximum flavor.

Incredible coconut milk

What did we do before we could buy canned coconut milk? It is a truly essential item in my pantry. It is wonderfully versatile, adding succulence to curries, a beautiful nutty taste to basmati rice and, of course, its delicious flavor to this sorbet recipe. It always needs to be whisked before use, as it often separates in the can into a thick paste and a watery liquid.

Orange sorbet

Sorbets are fantastically refreshing desserts that satisfy a sweet craving without making you feel overfull—and they are much easier to make than you might think, even without an ice cream machine. Give it a try and it will soon become part of your regular repertoire.

Makes about 2 pints
Preparation time 30 minutes,
    plus overnight freezing
Cooking time 5 minutes
Can be made in advance

1¾ cups superfine sugar
finely grated zest of 2 oranges (about 3 tbsp)
3 cups plus 3 tbsp fresh orange juice
juice of 1 lemon (about 3 tbsp)

1 Put the sugar into a pan with 1 cup cold water. Place over medium heat until all the sugar has dissolved. Add the orange zest, remove from the heat, and set aside to cool for 30 minutes.

2 Strain the mixture through a fine-mesh strainer to remove the orange zest, then add the orange and lemon juice. Stir together, pour the mixture into a lidded plastic container and place in the freezer for 45 minutes, or until it is beginning to freeze around the edges. Remove, spoon into a chilled bowl (or the bowl of a food processor), and beat until smooth and creamy. Repeat this freezing and beating process twice more (*see* secret, page 212), then return to the freezer until ready to serve. If using an ice-cream machine, churn for 1 hour instead, then turn into a lidded plastic container and store in the freezer.

3 Remove from the freezer at least 10 minutes before serving to soften slightly, for maximum flavor.

Organizing the freezer

Label all the items in your freezer with a marker pen or sticky labels; there's nothing worse than removing what you think is a delicious sorbet from the freezer 5 minutes before eating, then realizing—too late—that it is a batch of chicken stock! Try to make sure that plastic freezer containers are kept for either sweet or savory items to minimize the risk of aromas and tastes migrating. Onion-flavored sorbet, anybody…?

Raspberry sorbet

I have suggested using raspberries in this recipe, but you can use strawberries or blackberries instead, depending on the season. It is not necessary to strain the raspberry puree, as I do in step 2—it just depends on how you feel about seeds...

Makes about 2 pints
Preparation time 30 minutes,
    plus overnight freezing
Cooking time 5 minutes
Can be made in advance

2 cups superfine sugar
zest of 1 lemon (about 3 tsp), finely grated
1 quart raspberries
juice of 1 lemon (about 3 tbsp)

1 Put the sugar into a pan with 1 cup cold water and the lemon zest. Place over medium heat until all the sugar has dissolved, then remove from the heat. Strain to remove the lemon zest.

2 Reserve ¼ cup of the raspberries. Place the rest in a blender and process to a puree, then strain to remove the seeds. Add the puree to the syrup. Crush the reserved raspberries and add them too; I don't strain these as I like a few seeds in my sorbet. Add the lemon juice, stir, then set aside for 30 minutes to cool.

3 Spoon the mixture into a lidded plastic container and place in the freezer for 45 minutes, or until it is beginning to freeze around the edges. Remove, spoon into a chilled bowl (or the bowl of a food processor), and beat until smooth and creamy. Repeat this freezing and beating process twice more (*see* secret, page 212), then return to the freezer until ready to serve. If using an ice cream machine, churn for 1 hour instead, then turn into a lidded plastic container and store in the freezer.

4 Remove from the freezer at least 10 minutes before serving to soften slightly, for maximum flavor.

Scooping ice cream and sorbet
Move sorbet to the refrigerator to soften for 10 minutes before serving; move ice cream 20 minutes beforehand. When you're ready to eat, place 2 ice-cream scoops in a bowl of just-boiled water, as a warm scoop will both glide through sorbet or ice cream and release its load more readily. Using one, form an even ball. Place the ball in a dish or cone, then drop the used scoop back into the water and pick up the other scoop to continue.

Melon cooler

This is a very unusual dessert—a bit like a posh smoothie. If you are serving it to children, pour the melon "soup" into a mug, with the lovely strawberry salad at the bottom, and give them a teaspoon. This recipe makes a really fabulous end to a meal on a warm day.

Serves 2–4
Preparation time 15 minutes

1 ripe cantaloupe
6 basil leaves
6 tbsp crème fraîche
1 cup plain low-fat yogurt
2 ice cubes
4 large strawberries, cut into wedges
½ tbsp finely chopped mint
juice of 1 lime (about 2 tbsp)
zest of 1 lime (about 1 tsp), finely grated

1 Slice the melon in half and scoop out and discard the seeds. Remove the rind from one half, cut the flesh into chunks and place in a food processor with the basil, crème fraîche, yogurt, and ice cubes. Mix until smooth. Transfer to a pitcher and chill in the refrigerator until ready to serve.

2 Meanwhile, using a melon baller, make about 10 balls from the remaining melon. In a bowl, mix together the strawberries and melon balls, most of the mint, the lime juice, and most of the zest. Gently stir, taking care not to crush the strawberries.

3 Place a mound of fruit salad in a shallow bowl and gently pour the chilled melon "soup" around the outside. Finish by sprinkling with the remaining mint and zest.

Choosing melons

This recipe is worth making when you have a really tasty, wonderfully aromatic, ripe melon. Always smell a melon before you buy it to get a whiff of that wonderful scented muskiness. If there's no perfume, there will be no flavor. The best time of year to find perfectly ripe, sweet fruits is the summer, so eat this when the weather is hot and you're feeling frazzled.

Frozen fruit

This is my new favorite snack; it saves you from diving into packets of chips and is totally healthy! Frozen fruits are also an amazing after-dinner treat that will prevent you from reaching for yet more chocolates. Try this refreshing and zingy recipe once and you may find that you're totally hooked, too.

Serves 4 as a snack
Preparation time 10 minutes
Can be made in advance

½lb red grapes
½ pint blueberries
2 satsumas or small navel oranges, segmented
½lb pineapple, cubed

1 Freeze the fruit (*see* secret, below), then mix it up and put it into freezer bags in snack-size portions. Return to the freezer.

2 Remove the fruit from the freezer 10 minutes before eating, so it is not rock-hard. Simple as that!

How to freeze fruit

Freezing fruit maintains most of its nutritional value (and means you can enjoy seasonal treasures such as raspberries all year round). For the best results, place your prepared fruit in a single layer on a tray, cover with plastic wrap and place, flat, into the freezer. This way, the fruit will freeze individually and not stick together. When it is frozen solid, transfer the fruit into freezer bags for storage.

Pineapple with a lime twist

This guilt-free, easier-than-simple dessert takes minimum time and effort yet is cool, refreshing, and delicious! It's a great dish to serve with afternoon cocktails, or as a palate cleanser after a heavy, rich meal. Leave out the chile if you are serving this to children.

Serves 6
Preparation time 5–10 minutes
Can be made in advance

1 pineapple
zest of 1 lime (about 1 tsp), finely grated
½ red chile, seeded and very finely chopped
juice of 1 lime (about 2 tbsp)

1 Prepare the pineapple and cut into ¼–½in slices (*see* secret, below).

2 Arrange the pineapple slices on a plate. Sprinkle over the lime zest and chile, then squeeze over the lime juice. Cover and keep in the refrigerator for up to 24 hours before use. Remember to bring the pineapple to room temperature before serving.

Choosing and preparing pineapples

Buy your fruit perfectly ripe. Color is not always a sign of ripeness, so instead check the base: when pressed with a thumb it should "give" a little. Also, look at the leaves: if you can easily pull a leaf away from the fruit, it is ripe. To prepare the pineapple, cut off the stalk and base. Stand the pineapple upright on its newly flat base and remove the tough, leathery skin using a sharp knife—I find a serrated breadknife useful. Then cut out all the "eyes"—the regular indentations of hard skin—and cut the flesh into slices or chunks, as preferred. If the central core is hard, cut it out from each slice and discard.

Mango & passion fruit dessert

It doesn't get any simpler or tastier than this. You could try this dessert with a light sorbet on the side if you wanted to jazz it up a bit, but I think it is truly refreshing left as it is. Look for passion fruit in Latin markets.

Serves 4
Preparation time 10 minutes
Can be made in advance

1 large ripe mango, peeled and thinly sliced
  (*see* secret, below)
4 passion fruit
finely grated zest of 2 limes (about 2 tsp)
10 mint leaves, finely chopped

1 Divide the mango slices between 4 serving plates. Halve the passion fruit, scoop out the pulp and seeds and drizzle them over the mango.

2 Sprinkle the lime zest and mint over the top, then serve.

Preparing mangoes

This is easy once you get the hang of it. Each mango has an oval, flat pit. Pick up the fruit and look at the stem end: the pit runs along the longest axis. Cut either side of the pit to remove the 2 "cheeks" of the mango, then peel it. The remaining flesh clinging to the pit is a harder prospect: just hack away as much of it as you can! Work over a bowl, to catch the lovely juices.

Caramelized peaches with hazelnut crème fraîche

This is a simple but impressive dessert that you can pretty much produce from pantry ingredients—you can even use canned peaches! For a nice change, roll the peach segments in sliced, toasted almonds at the end of step 2 and serve with plain crème fraîche.

Serves 4
Preparation time 10 minutes
Cooking time 10–15 minutes

⅓ cup superfine sugar
1 tbsp unsalted butter
3 peaches, pitted, each cut into 6 wedges
½ cup white wine

To serve
3 tbsp crème fraîche
¼ cup chopped lightly toasted hazelnuts

1 Pour the sugar into a pan set over medium heat and allow it to caramelize, watching constantly so it doesn't burn (*see* secret, page 145). Add the butter, keeping the pan moving until it is melted and you have a lovely, rich brown glossy liquid.

2 Add the peach segments and toss so they are all coated with the caramel, then pour in the wine. Allow the liquid to bubble and reduce by half.

3 Meanwhile mix the crème fraîche with the chopped hazelnuts.

4 Divide the peach segments between 4 small serving bowls, drizzling a spoonful of their liquid over the top. Serve accompanied by the hazelnut crème fraîche.

How to toast nuts

Pour your nuts into a dry skillet over medium heat. Stir and toss them, so all sides are evenly roasted, watching constantly as they can scorch in an instant and become acrid. When they are ready they will smell delicious and appear golden brown. Transfer them to a plate to cool before serving; if you leave them in their pan they may well burn in the residual heat.

Apricot, raspberry, & ginger crumble

When I was at school, crumbles were my favorite desserts, and they have been ever since. This is a great way to use up over-ripe fruit. When you are feeling decadent, pour heavy cream over the top, or serve with a spoon of ice cream, or even crème fraîche.

Serves 4–6
Preparation time 15 minutes
Cooking time 40–45 minutes
Can be made in advance
Suitable for freezing

2 tbsp unsalted butter
1lb 9oz apricots, halved and pitted
leaves from 2 thyme sprigs
⅓ cup superfine sugar
1 pint raspberries

For the crumble
1¼ cups all-purpose flour
½ cup light brown sugar
½ tsp ginger
½ tsp ground cloves
½ tsp cinnamon
¼ cup hazelnuts, chopped
6 tbsp unsalted butter

1 Preheat the oven to 350°F.

2 Melt the butter in a large skillet over low heat and add the apricots and thyme. Toss to coat in the butter and leave to heat through for a couple of minutes. Stir in the superfine sugar and leave to bubble gently for 10–15 minutes, or until the apricots are softened but not breaking down.

3 Transfer the apricots to an ovenproof dish and sprinkle the raspberries evenly over the top.

4 Mix together the flour, light brown sugar, ginger, cloves, cinnamon, and nuts for the crumble in a large bowl. Cut in the butter in knobs and rub with your fingertips until the mixture resembles bread crumbs. Sprinkle the crumble over the top of the fruit.

5 Place the crumble dish on a baking sheet and cook in the oven for 30 minutes, until golden and bubbling.

Saving apricots

Very sadly, unless you live close to where apricots are grown, you are likely to come across only disappointing fruits with a dry, woolly texture. Some, by contrast, will be mouth-puckeringly acidic. But you can save them by baking them, as in this recipe, or poaching them in a rosewater-flavored syrup and serving with raspberry sauce. They can even be made into chutney.

Plum & almond pudding

This recipe works well with cherries, rhubarb, or apple instead of plums, or you could even use canned or frozen fruit. Change the fruit to suit the season, your budget, and your tastes. Serve with vanilla ice cream, or just dig in as it is.

Serves 6
Preparation time 10 minutes
Cooking time 40–50 minutes

2 tbsp butter
8 plums, pitted and cut into quarters
½ cup light brown sugar
3 eggs
½ cup superfine sugar
⅔ cup tsp self-rising flour
⅔ cup tsp ground almonds
1 cup plus 2 tbsp low-fat milk
few drops of almond extract
2 tbsp sliced almonds

1 Preheat the oven to 350°F.

2 Melt the butter in a large skillet over medium heat, add the plums and light brown sugar and cook for 6–8 minutes until the plums have softened. Tip the plums and their juices into a 7-cup ovenproof dish, making sure there's enough room for the fruit to lie in a single layer.

3 Meanwhile, whisk the eggs and superfine sugar together until pale in color and thick enough for the whisk to leave a trail on the surface. Carefully beat in the flour, ground almonds, milk, and almond extract. Spoon the mixture over the plums and sprinkle with the sliced almonds.

4 Bake in the oven for 35–40 minutes, or until the pudding is golden brown and set. After 20 minutes, check the top has not browned too much; if it has, cover it with foil and return to the oven for the remaining cooking time.

Respect the seasons

When making this or any other fruit pudding, select your fruit to suit the season. Seasonal fruit will be the ripest and at the peak of its flavor. It will also be sold at its most economical price.

Pear & ginger steamed sponge pudding

This takes a while to cook, so prepare it in advance and leave it to putter away on the stove. Despite what you may imagine, this is a light dessert (though it is also wonderfully syrupy around the rim—that's the bit to fight over!). Perfect served with custard, or just on its own.

Serves 6
Preparation time 20 minutes
Cooking time 2 hours 10 minutes

knob of butter (about 2 tbsp)
2 tbsp superfine sugar
2 ripe pears, peeled, cored, and diced
½ cup Calvados
2 tbsp crystallized ginger, finely chopped
12 tbsp (1½ sticks) unsalted butter, softened, plus extra for the basin
¾ cup granulated sugar
3 eggs, beaten
1¼ cups self-rising flour

1 Place a sauté pan over medium heat, add the butter and superfine sugar and toss in the diced pears to coat. Standing well back, pour in the Calvados. Then add the ginger, stir and allow to bubble for 5 minutes. Transfer the pears to a plate and set aside to cool.

2 Cream together the butter and granulated sugar, using the paddle attachment of an electric mixer or by hand (*see* secret, page 246). Add the eggs a little at a time, beating after each addition, then fold in the flour with the cooled pears.

3 Butter a 6-cup pudding mold well. Spoon in the batter and smooth the top. Steam for up to 2 hours (follow the instructions in the secret, below left), making sure to top off the water so the pan does not run dry. To serve, turn out the sponge onto a plate.

How to steam a pudding

Cut both a piece of aluminum foil and a piece of parchment paper bigger than the top of the pudding mold (or just use a double thickness of parchment paper). Put them together and pleat the center so the pudding has room to expand. Butter the paper and place it and the foil over the mold, buttered paper side down, tie string around to secure and make 2 string handles so the pudding is easier to remove from the steamer. Place a steamer over a pan of boiling water and lower in the pudding. Cover with a tight-fitting lid.

Homemade ginger lemonade

A good way to come across as the perfect mother is to turn up for the Little League game with homemade lemonade. For an extra kick, serve with a shot of vodka. For parents only, of course!

Serves 6
Preparation time 10 minutes,
   plus 4 hours infusing
Can be made in advance

3¼in piece fresh ginger,
   peeled and very finely sliced
freshly squeezed juice of 6 lemons
   (about 1 cup), plus 1 lemon, thinly sliced
4½ tbsp granulated sugar
handful of fresh mint leaves, to decorate

1 Place the ginger, lemon juice, sliced lemon, and sugar in a tall heatproof pitcher and add 5½ cups of boiling water. Stir and leave to cool, then cover and transfer to the refrigerator to infuse for at least 4 hours, or for as long as possible.

2 When the lemonade is ready to serve, pass the mixture through a fine-mesh strainer into a clean pitcher. Dilute with an equal part of water and serve with plenty of ice and the mint leaves.

How to choose and juice a lemon

Look for lemons with smooth, oily skins. They should be heavy for their size as the weightiest fruits will contain the most juice. Whole lemons will keep for 1–2 weeks at room temperature, but longer in the refrigerator. To extract the most juice from a fruit, use your palm to roll it firmly on a hard surface to loosen the fibers within. If you need only a little juice, pierce the end of the fruit with a fork, squeeze out the amount needed, wrap the remaining lemon in plastic wrap, and pop it back in the refrigerator for later.

Cherry & chocolate mousse

This is an easy-yet-impressive, light and airy dessert that you can whip up in advance. I use fresh cherries in this recipe, but I've also had a great deal of success with canned fruits when they're out of season, so don't just keep this dish for the summer months.

Makes 6 cocktail glasses
Preparation time 15 minutes,
   plus 30 minutes chilling
Cooking time 10 minutes
Can be made in advance

¾ cup granulated sugar
1lb cherries, halved and stoned

For the mousse
5oz dark chocolate, plus extra
   to grate on top
2¼ cups low-fat crème fraîche
1 cup heavy cream, whipped to soft peaks

1 Put the sugar into a pan with ½ cup cold water. Place over low heat until all the sugar has dissolved. Toss in the cherries, increase the heat, and boil for about 5 minutes, or until the juices are syrupy and they coat the cherries. Transfer the cherries and juices into a bowl and set aside to cool.

2 Meanwhile, melt the chocolate (follow the instructions in the secret, below left), then allow it to cool slightly. Gently stir in the crème fraîche and heavy cream.

3 Divide the cherry mixture between 6 cocktail glasses. Spoon the chocolate mousse on top of each and refrigerate for at least 30 minutes to chill and slightly set. Grate on top a little more chocolate just before serving.

How to melt chocolate

Break the chocolate into chunks and place it in a heatproof bowl fitted over a pan of simmering water over gentle heat, making sure the base of the bowl doesn't touch the water. Stir the chocolate only now and again and allow it to melt gently. If it becomes grainy or separates (known as "seizing"), it has been over-heated. To rescue it, stir in 1 tsp vegetable oil.

Chocolate cheesecake

This is simple, delicious, and very quick. Don't be worried that it might take you all day and involve using all the mixing bowls you own. Give it a go and it will soon become part of your regular repertoire.

Serves 8–10
Preparation time 15 minutes
Cooking time 1 hour
Can be made in advance

10½oz package oatmeal cookies
6 tbsp butter, melted
5½oz good-quality dark chocolate,
    broken into squares
1lb 10oz mascarpone or cream cheese
2/3 cup light brown sugar
3 eggs, beaten

1 Preheat the oven to 350°F. Line a 9in nonstick springform pan with parchment paper.

2 Put the cookies in a food processor and process until they are in fine crumbs (or put them in a plastic bag, seal and bash with a rolling pin). Place them in a large bowl, add the butter and stir until they are evenly coated. Transfer to the lined pan and press firmly with the back of a spoon to compress in an even layer over the base. Cover with plastic wrap and put in the refrigerator for 10–15 minutes, until hardened.

3 Meanwhile, melt the chocolate (*see* secret, page 233). Remove from the heat and set aside to cool.

4 Put the mascarpone in another mixing bowl and, with a whisk, beat until loose and smooth. Add the sugar and beat again. Gently stir in the cooled chocolate and the eggs, then pour this onto the chilled cookie base.

5 Gently slide the cheesecake into the oven and bake for 50–60 minutes. When it's ready, it should still have a wobble to the center if you shake the pan (it will continue to cook as it cools). Set aside to cool completely, then refrigerate until ready to serve.

Why use brown sugar?

In this recipe I use light brown, which is a truly delicious sugar. It has a rich flavor, which comes from the molasses syrup clinging to the grains. Refined white sugar has a less interesting taste, as all this molasses has been removed, so it is simply sweet without much depth. Use brown sugar when you can; it will give your desserts real depth of flavor.

Simple Champagne cocktail

Champagne comes from the eponymous French region and is the classic choice for this drink, but use more economical sparkling wine here if you want to. Just be careful that it's a nice bottle, taking advice from a trusted wine merchant, to avoid cheap plonk.

Serves 4–6
Preparation time 5 minutes

2 passion fruits
1 bottle of your favorite Champagne
   or sparkling wine, chilled

1 Cut the passion fruits in half and scrape out all the seeds and pulp into a bowl.

2 Spoon 1 tsp passion fruit seeds into the bottom of each Champagne glass and divide the juices between them as well.

3 Pour Champagne over the passion fruit and serve immediately.

The right shape for Champagne glasses

Although the shallow, wide bowl of a Champagne *coupe* is attractive and remains popular in television costume dramas, it is really not the best vessel for your bubbly. A tall, slim flute will keep the drink fizzier, as the smaller surface area means there is less room for the bubbles to rise and escape. A flute will also save you the embarrassment of spluttering after bubbles have gone up your nose!

Cakes & cookies

Raspberry & lemon torta · Victoria sponge · Cherry & almond loaf

Cupcake party time · Chocolate heaven cupcakes

Garibaldi cookies · Apple & raspberry crumb muffins

Carrot & raisin cupcakes · Chocolate, fruit, & nut cookies

Lemon & thyme shortbread · Gingerbread men & hearts

Secrets of baking cakes & cookies

A lot of people are coming back to baking. As long as you follow the rules and measure things out accurately, it's easy. And you'll know exactly what your family is eating when you've made the cakes yourself. It's a really homey, satisfying feeling to bake your own.

I love making cookies and that's the sort of homebaking I do the most. I tend to make three times the recipe and store the dough in sausage-shapes wrapped in plastic wrap in the refrigerator or freezer. This way, it takes an instant to impress people with freshly baked cookies when they come to visit, or welcome the kids home to the smell of baking on a Friday evening.

Be brave and use unusual combinations of flavors in your baking. My Lemon & Thyme Shortbread (*see* page 264), for instance, may sound eccentric, but it tastes divine. Try the recipe with cinnamon instead, or even very finely chopped rosemary. You should always experiment in the kitchen, but don't be afraid to raise your hands and admit that something was a terrible combination and never try it again!

Having experienced the competitive pressures of school bake sales, I have decided that the only way to go is to find a recipe that no one else will know or, at least, to claim that what you have brought along is a unique cake. That way no one can say theirs is better than yours, or that you have messed up the baking!

Cupcakes (*see* pages 250, 254, and 260) will get you out of all sorts of holes. You can make them as glamorous as you like for a tea party, create individual cakes for each child, or even get the children to make their own designs. Just remember they are best eaten on the day they are made.

Muffins (*see* page 257) are amazingly handy, and are a good breakfast on the run for you or your children.

Raspberry & lemon torta

This torta is at its delicious best when served slightly warm. It does sink a little in the middle but this recipe is all about taste, not looks. It will last a couple of days, which is always handy. And I do love raspberries!

Serves 8
Preparation time 10 minutes
Cooking time 1 hour
Can be made in advance

8 tbsp (1 stick) unsalted butter, melted and
    cooled, plus extra for the pan
2 pints raspberries
juice of ½ lemon (about 1½ tbsp)
1 cup light brown sugar, plus extra
    for the top
3 eggs
1¾ cups all-purpose flour, sifted
2 rounded tsp baking powder
finely grated zest of 1 lemon (about 3 tsp)

1 Preheat the oven to 325°F. Butter an 8in round cake pan and line the base with parchment paper.

2 Place the raspberries and lemon juice in a mixing bowl. In another large bowl, whisk together the sugar and eggs until pale and thick, then carefully fold in the flour, baking powder, and lemon zest. Gently stir in the butter.

3 Pour the batter into the pan, then scatter in the raspberries and their juices. Sprinkle a little sugar over the top.

4 Bake for 1 hour, or until the cake springs back to the touch (*see* secret, below). Check the *torta* halfway through the cooking time—you may find you need to cover it with foil to prevent the top from scorching. Allow to cool in the pan, before removing to a cooling rack.

How to know when a cake is cooked
When a cake is cooked it will have an even color, will be firm yet springy to the touch, and should be slightly pulling away from the edges of the pan. Insert a clean toothpick or skewer right down into its center. If it comes out clean, the cake is done. After removing it from the oven, give it a few minutes to rest in its pan before turning out onto a cooling rack.

Victoria sponge

A classic English dessert and a guilty pleasure, this is one of my favorite cakes. It's perfect with a cup of tea! I like raspberry jam as it's a little more tart than most other jams, but do use strawberry jam if you like a sweeter filling.

Makes 8 slices
Preparation time 10 minutes,
    plus 2 hours cooling
Cooking time 20–25 minutes
Can be made in advance
Suitable for freezing

1 cup (2 sticks) unsalted butter, softened,
    plus extra for the pan
1½ cups superfine sugar
3 eggs, lightly beaten
1½ cups self-rising flour
2 tbsp milk

For the butter frosting
1¼ cups confectioners' sugar, sifted,
    plus 1 tsp extra to dust
6 tbsp unsalted butter, softened
6 tbsp raspberry or strawberry jam

1 Preheat the oven to 350°F. Butter two 8-in cake tins and line the bases with parchment paper.

2 Cream together the butter and superfine sugar, using the paddle attachment of an electric stand mixer or by hand (*see* secret, below). Add the eggs a little at a time, beating after each addition. Fold in the flour (*see* secret, page 254). Stir in the milk until the batter falls easily from a spoon.

3 Divide the batter evenly between the prepared cake pans and bake for 20–25 minutes, until the cakes are golden brown and a toothpick inserted into the center comes out clean. Remove from the oven and, as soon as you can handle the pans, turn out onto a wire rack and let cool completely.

4 To make the frosting, beat the confectioners' sugar and butter together in a large bowl until smooth and creamy. Spread a thick layer over the top of whichever cake has emerged from the oven looking less picturesque. Spread the jam over the base of the other half. Sandwich together the cakes. Place 1 tsp confectioners' sugar into a fine-mesh strainer and dust over the cake before serving.

How to cream a cake batter

Start with butter at room temperature, so you can work with it easily. If you have an electric mixer, creaming is easy, otherwise elbow grease works wonders! Beat the butter with the sugar for about 5 minutes, or until very light, pale, and fluffy. Add the eggs a little at a time, beating well after each addition. If the mixture curdles, beat in 1 tbsp flour to bring it back together.

Cherry & almond loaf

This recipe belongs to my mother-in-law, Helen, and my son Jack thinks it is the best cake EVER... It is fantastic for a couple of days after baking as long as you keep it in an airtight container or wrap it in foil.

Makes 10 slices
Preparation time 10 minutes
Cooking time 50–55 minutes
Can be made in advance
Suitable for freezing

12 tbsp (1½ sticks) unsalted butter, softened,
   plus extra for the pan
1¼ cups superfine sugar
finely grated zest of 1 lemon (about 3 tsp)
   and juice of ½ lemon (about 1½ tbsp)
3 eggs, beaten
1 cup candied cherries, rinsed and halved
²/₃ cup tsp self-rising flour, sifted
²/₃ cup tsp all-purpose flour, sifted
pinch of salt
²/₃ cup tsp ground almonds
splash of milk (optional)

1 Preheat the oven to 375°F. Butter a 9 × 5 × 3in loaf pan, then line it with parchment paper (*see* secret, below).

2 Cream together the butter, sugar, lemon zest, and juice, using the paddle attachment of an electric mixer or by hand (*see* secret, page 246). Add the eggs a little at a time, beating after each addition.

3 Toss the cherries in a little of the flour to help them cling to the cake mixture instead of dropping to the bottom. Next, mix together the flours, salt, almonds, and cherries and add to the batter, stirring well until the cherries are evenly distributed. The cake mixture needs to be fairly stiff, but add a splash of milk if you feel you need to.

4 Bake for 50–55 minutes, then test for doneness by inserting a skewer into the loaf's center; if it comes out clean, it is done. If you find the top is browning too much before the loaf is ready, simply cover with foil and let it carry on baking.

5 Remove from the pan to a wire rack, leaving it in the parchment paper until cooled.

Lining a cake pan
Using the pan as a template, cut out 2 strips of parchment paper. One should be the width of the pan's base and longer than the base and sides together, the other the length of the pan's base, again longer than the base and sides. Butter the pan and line it with the parchment paper, leaving overhanging pieces on each side to act as handles when the loaf is finished baking.

Cupcake party time

Taking cupcakes into school for the annual bake sale is the highlight of the year for our kids. That is, of course, when they remember to tell me they're needed in time! For this recipe you'll need 20 paper baking cups.

Makes 20 cakes
Preparation time 20 minutes
Cooking time 15 minutes
Can be made in advance

12 tbsp (1½ sticks) unsalted butter, softened
1¼ cups superfine sugar
2 large eggs, beaten
1 tsp vanilla extract
1¼ cups self-rising flour, sifted

For the icing
2 cups confectioners' sugar, sifted
2 drops red food coloring (optional)

For the decorations (optional)
mini marshmallows
white chocolate chips
multicolored sprinkles
silver sprinkles

The best glaze icing

Glaze icing should have a fairly stiff consistency after the water is added; if it doesn't, add more sugar until it does! If you use hot water you will get a shinier icing that's less likely to crack when it sets. It should be thick enough to leave a trail when trickled from a spoon back into the bowl. Replace some of the water with a squeeze of lemon or orange juice if you want a more flavorsome icing.

1 Preheat the oven to 350°F.

2 Cream together the butter and superfine sugar, using the paddle attachment of an electric mixer or by hand, until pale and fluffy (*see* secret, page 246). Add the eggs a little at a time, beating after each addition, then stir in the vanilla extract and fold in the flour (*see* secret, page 254).

3 Place the paper baking cups into a cupcake tray and fill each halfway full with the cake batter. Don't be tempted to overfill them as they will turn into a mess instead of a neatly contained cupcake.

4 Bake for 15 minutes, or until the cakes are golden and spring back to the touch.

5 Remove to a wire rack and leave until cold. (Do not try to ice the cakes until they are cold—it would be a disaster!)

6 To make the icing, place the confectioners' sugar in a large bowl and beat in 3 tbsp water and the food coloring, if using (*see* secret, left).

7 Smooth the icing over the cakes with an offset spatula, being generous. While the icing is still wet, sprinkle or arrange on any decorations that you or your child desire. Set aside to allow the icing to set.

8 All that is left to do now is to place the cakes carefully onto a cake stand and avoid dropping them on the way into school!

Chocolate heaven cupcakes

The pink Cupcake Party Time creations, with their sparkly sprinkles (see page 250), are far removed from anything my son would be seen taking into school. His idea of cupcakes is anything with chocolate, chocolate, and more chocolate. For this recipe you'll need 18 paper baking cups.

Makes 18 cakes
Preparation time 20 minutes
Cooking time 15 minutes
Can be made in advance

12 tbsp (1½ sticks) unsalted butter, softened
1¼ cups superfine sugar
2 large eggs, beaten
1¼ cups self-rising flour, sifted
2 tbsp cocoa powder, sifted
white chocolate disks, to decorate

For the butter frosting
8 tbsp (1 stick) unsalted butter, softened
1¼ cups confectioners' sugar, sifted
3½ tbsp cocoa powder, sifted

How to fold in flour

After you have creamed together butter and sugar for a cake batter and added the eggs gradually, you need to retain the air thus created in the mixture to give the cakes their final lightness. To do so, sift the flour and fold it into the batter lightly, using a figure-of-eight motion and being careful not to beat out the air. Make sure that all traces of dry flour are well blended into the batter.

1 Preheat the oven to 350°F.

2 Cream together the butter and superfine sugar, using the paddle attachment of an electric mixer or by hand, until pale and fluffy (see secret, page 246). Add the eggs a little at a time, beating after each addition. Fold in the flour and cocoa powder (see secret, below left).

3 Place the paper baking cups in a cupcake tray and fill each halfway full with the mixture. Don't be tempted to overfill them as they will turn into a mess instead of a neatly contained cupcake.

4 Bake for 15 minutes, or until the cakes are well risen and spring back to the touch. Remove to a wire rack and leave to cool completely.

5 To make the butter frosting, place the butter, confectioners' sugar, and cocoa, along with 2 tbsp water, in an electric stand mixer with a whisk attachment, or into a large bowl (be prepared to use lots of elbow grease if you don't have electric beaters). Whisk for 5–10 minutes—the longer, the better—to give the frosting lots of volume. It will become deliciously light and glossy.

6 Generously spread the frosting onto the cupcakes with an offset spatula. Decorate with white chocolate disks.

Garibaldi cookies

Garibaldi cookies were my favorites growing up, with their thin glazed cookie exterior and squashed currant filling. My brothers called them squashed-fly cookies and could never understand why I loved them so much. This is the closest I can get to a replica and is equally delicious. I have played around, adding lemon or orange zest, but the original version beats all.

Makes 20 cookies
Preparation time 20 minutes
Cooking time 15–20 minutes
Can be made in advance

1½ cups all-purpose flour
2 tbsp cornstarch
¼ cup superfine sugar
pinch of salt
4 tbsp (½ stick) butter, softened
1 egg, separated
½ cup milk
confectioners' sugar, to dust
²/₃ cup currants

1 Preheat the oven to 375°F.

2 Sift the flour and cornstarch into a large bowl and stir in the sugar and salt. Cut in the butter in knobs and rub in with your fingertips until the mixture resembles bread crumbs. Add the egg yolk and milk, and mix it all together to form a stiff dough.

3 Lightly dust a clean, dry work surface with confectioners' sugar, dust your rolling pin too, and roll out the dough into a 12 × 8in rectangle. Sprinkle the currants onto one half. Fold over the other half of the dough to cover the fruit and gently push together, sealing the edges by squashing them. Roll over the top with the rolling pin until the dough is about ¼in thick, then cut into the traditional rectangles, each about 2½ × 1¼in in size. Prick each all over with a fork.

4 Line a baking sheet with parchment paper and spread the cookies over it. Brush the top of each with the egg white and bake for 15–20 minutes, or until golden brown. Remove from the oven and carefully transfer to a wire rack, using an offset spatula, then set aside until cold. Sift a little confectioners' sugar on top to serve.

Storing cakes and cookies

To keep cookies and cakes fresh, seal them in an airtight container. An old cookie or mixed chocolates tin is good for this. Always store them at room temperature, not in the refrigerator, to keep them tasting fresh and feeling crisp. Do not keep cookies and cakes for more than a week, as they will be past their best.

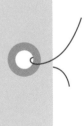

Apple & raspberry crumb muffins

You will need a 12-hole muffin pan (which has deeper holes than a cupcake pan) and, ideally, some paper baking cups. If you don't have baking cups, see my secret, on page 260. The apple keeps these muffins very moist and this recipe is a handy way to use up those that are past their best.

Makes 12 muffins
Preparation time 15 minutes
Cooking time 30–35 minutes
Can be made in advance

3 eggs
¾ cup crème fraîche
1¾ cups superfine sugar
1½ cups all-purpose flour, sifted
1½ tsp baking powder
1 apple, peeled, cored, and finely chopped
1 cup raspberries

For the crumb topping
4 tbsp (½ stick) unsalted butter, diced
⅓ cup all-purpose flour
2 tbsp light brown sugar
1 tbsp roasted, chopped hazelnuts

1 Preheat the oven to 340°F.

2 First make the crumb topping using the butter and flour (*see* secret, below). Stir in the light brown sugar and hazelnuts. Set aside.

3 Place the eggs, crème fraîche, superfine sugar, flour, and baking powder into a bowl and mix together until smooth. Add the apple and half the raspberries and stir through, taking care not to crush the raspberries.

4 Place the paper baking cups into a muffin pan and fill halfway with the batter. Stir the remaining raspberries into the crumb topping and spoon this evenly on top.

5 Bake the muffins for 30–35 minutes, until golden and cooked through. When ready, they should spring back to the touch. Remove from the oven and allow to cool in the pan. These keep very well for a couple of days in an airtight container—the apple helps to keep the cake really moist.

How to make a crumb topping
When making crumb topping, be sure you use cold butter. Add it to the flour and rub together very lightly with your fingertips, until the mixture resembles fine bread crumbs and all the large lumps of butter have dispersed evenly. The warmth of your hands will soften the butter enough to blend with the flour. Stir in the remaining flavorings and the sugar. Don't overwork the topping, or it will be heavy and clumpy.

Carrot & raisin cupcakes

These cupcakes don't contain much fat but, of course, they contain vegetables, so they are relatively healthy...for cakes, at least! They provide the perfect energy boost between meals—just try not to eat too many! For this recipe, you will need a 12-hole cupcake pan and, ideally, some paper baking cups.

Makes 12 cakes
Preparation time 20 minutes
Cooking time 30 minutes
Can be made in advance

3 tbsp raisins
grated zest of 1 orange (about 1½ tbsp)
juice of 1 orange (about ½ cup)
4 eggs, separated
1 cup brown sugar
1¾ cups ground walnuts
1 tsp ground cinnamon
1½ cups carrots, grated
1¼ cups whole-wheat flour
1 tsp baking powder

For the icing
8oz cream cheese
²/₃ cup confectioners' sugar, sifted
juice of 1 orange (about ½ cup)
grated zest of 1 orange (about 1½ tbsp)

1 Preheat the oven to 350°F.

2 Place the raisins in a bowl with the orange zest and juice and leave to plump up for 10 minutes, or longer if you have the time.

3 Whisk together the egg yolks and brown sugar until thick and creamy. Add all the remaining ingredients except the egg whites and fold through until the mixture is nice and smooth. Beat the egg whites until they form stiff peaks when you remove the whisk, then carefully fold them into the cake mixture.

4 Place the baking cups into a cupcake pan and divide the batter between them. Bake the cupcakes in the oven for 30 minutes, until well risen and golden brown. Remove from the oven, place on a cooling rack, and leave to cool completely.

5 Meanwhile, prepare the icing. Beat the cream cheese in a large bowl with the confectioners' sugar until smooth. Add enough orange juice to reach your preferred consistency. Spread the icing over each cupcake and sprinkle with the orange zest.

Homemade cupcake cases
If you don't have any paper baking cups, cut suitably-sized disks of waxed paper or parchment paper and use them to line the cups in your cupcake pan instead.

Chocolate, fruit, & nut cookies

Based on my favorite chocolate bar—fruit and nut—these cookies are a fantastic energy boost. Well, that's my excuse! Do experiment with this recipe; try replacing the milk chocolate with white, for instance, or using dried cranberries in place of the raisins.

Makes 35 cookies
Preparation time 10 minutes,
 plus 2 hours chilling
Cooking time 15–20 minutes
Can be made in advance

14 tbsp unsalted butter, softened
1¼ cups light brown sugar
2 eggs, beaten
2 cups all-purpose flour, sifted,
 plus extra to dust
1 tsp baking soda
½ cup hazelnuts, lightly crushed
5½oz milk chocolate,
 in hazelnut-size chunks
⅔ cup raisins

1 Cream together the butter and sugar, using the paddle attachment of a hand-held electric mixer or by hand (*see* secret, page 246). Add the eggs a little at a time, beating after each addition, then fold in the flour and baking soda. Stir in the hazelnuts, chocolate, and raisins.

2 Flour a work surface and tip out the dough. Break it into 3 even-size pieces and work each into a long sausage shape about 1½–2in in diameter. Wrap tightly in plastic wrap and refrigerate for a couple of hours (*see* secret, below left).

3 When you are ready to bake the cookies, preheat the oven to 350°F. Line 2 baking sheets with parchment paper.

4 Remove the dough from the refrigerator and unwrap the plastic wrap. Slice the dough sausages into ½in wide slices and space them out well on the baking sheets they will each spread about ½–¾in all around). Bake the cookies for 15–20 minutes, or until golden brown. When they are done, transfer them immediately to a wire rack to stop the bottoms from burning.

Working with cookie dough

Make sure the dough is not too wet or dry, or it will be difficult to shape into cookies. As you practice, you will learn when to add more flour to a too-sticky dough, or milk to a dry mixture. Always refrigerate cookie dough before cooking; this helps to firm it up and stops the cookies spreading into one big flat mess in the oven.

Lemon & thyme shortbread

I have suggested thyme for these delicate cookies, but you can always substitute lemon thyme if you are lucky enough to find it. Many supermarkets now stock it, so be sure to look out for it in the herb section. It will give the cookies a more tangy flavor.

Makes about 48 cookies
Preparation time 15 minutes,
   plus 2 hours chilling
Cooking time 10–15 minutes
Can be made in advance

3 cups plus 1 tbsp all-purpose flour
2 tsp baking powder
pinch of salt
2 tbsp finely chopped thyme leaves
1 cup (2 sticks) unsalted butter, softened
1⅓ cups light brown sugar
2 tbsp finely grated lemon zest
1 egg, beaten
juice of 1 small lemon (about 3 tbsp)

Successful shortbread

I like flaky, light shortbread, not old-fashioned heavy slabs, so I cut the cookies quite thin. It is important to refrigerate the dough until it feels really firm. If you chill it in the roll shape that I suggest in this recipe and store in the refrigerator, you will also be ready simply to slice it into cookies and impress guests with warm shortbread in just 15 minutes.

1 Sift the flour and baking powder into a large bowl and stir in the salt and thyme.

2 Cream together the butter, sugar, and lemon zest, using the paddle attachment of a hand-held electric mixer or by hand, until pale and fluffy (*see* secret, page 246). Add the egg a little at a time, beating after each addition, then slowly add the dry ingredients, stirring in well and drizzling in a little lemon juice until it comes together as dough. Do not add too much juice as the dough should not be too wet.

3 Roll the dough into 2 sausage shapes each about 2in in diameter. This way, each will make a batch of 24 cookies, so you could choose to save one batch for another time. Wrap each sausage tightly in plastic wrap and refrigerate for at least 2 hours, or up to 2 days.

4 When you are ready to bake the shortbread, preheat the oven to 375°F. Line a baking sheet with parchment paper.

5 Unwrap the plastic wrap and slice the roll of dough into ¼in thick cookies. Spread these out on the baking sheet and bake for 10–15 minutes, until the cookies are very slightly tinged with gold at the edges. Remove from the oven and carefully transfer to a wire rack, using an offset spatula, then allow to cool completely.

Gingerbread men & hearts

My children love these. Hearts and gingerbread men are my favorite cutter shapes and I find the sight of these cookies enormously comforting. At Christmas time, try hanging a batch on the tree. Make sure they are eaten soon (that shouldn't be a problem!) or they will lose their crunch.

Makes 25 cookies
Preparation time 10–15 minutes
Cooking time 12 minutes
Can be made in advance
Suitable for freezing at end of step 4

2½ cups all-purpose flour, plus extra to dust
1 tsp ginger
½ tsp ground cloves
½ tsp cinnamon
1 tsp baking soda
1¼ cups brown sugar
7 tbsp unsalted butter, softened
1 egg
4 tbsp dark corn syrup
splash of milk (optional)
1¼ cups confectioners' sugar, sifted
2 tbsp currants or raisins (optional)

Ground spices— the little and often rule

Spices are at their best when freshly ground and lose their fragrance and potency very quickly. To avoid dusty, tasteless spices, avoid buying them in large quantities. Instead, go for the smallest packages you can find and use them up soon after purchase. Any that you find hidden at the back of a shelf (and there will be the odd jar!) are best replaced with a fresh batch.

1 Preheat the oven to 350°F.

2 Mix together the flour, ginger, ground cloves, cinnamon, baking soda, and brown sugar in a large bowl, then cut in the butter in knobs and rub it in with your fingertips until the mixture resembles bread crumbs.

3 Whisk together the egg and corn syrup and add to the dry ingredients, then knead until it forms a dough. You may need to add a very little milk, but the dough should not be wet or sticky.

4 Flour a work surface well and roll out the dough to ¼in thick. Choose some gingerbread men cutters —mine are about 3in long—and some heart shapes, and use to cut the dough.

5 Evenly space the gingerbread shapes on a baking sheet lined with parchment paper and bake for 12 minutes, or until golden brown. Remove from the oven, carefully transfer to a wire rack with an offset spatula and allow to cool completely.

6 Mix the confectioners' sugar with about 2 tbsp cold water to make a fairly thick icing that will coat the back of a spoon. Decorate the gingerbreads with the icing and add currant or raisin eyes, or buttons, to the man shapes if you like.

Sauces & dressings

Tomato & tarragon mayonnaise · Chile & lime mayonnaise
Cheese dip · Creamy mustard vinaigrette
Homemade ranch-style dressing · Tomato sauce · Tomato salsa
Creamy corn salsa · Chunky apple sauce · Homemade gravy

Secrets of making sauces & dressings

Obviously, you can buy all your dressings, sauces, and gravies in bottles at the supermarket. But I bet, if you read the labels, you'll be surprised by some of the ingredients. Do you really want to eat something if you can't understand what it is?

I strongly recommend you make your own mayonnaise. It's so satisfying to do and tastes wickedly delicious and indulgent. And it's not difficult to do. Just follow my instructions (*see* pages 272 and 274) and enjoy the process. Once you have tasted the incredible difference between this and shop-bought mayo, you'll never look back.

Homemade Ranch-style Dressing (*see* page 277) is a wonder condiment in our house. It's a great compromise between the simple vinaigrettes that I love and the creamier sauces that are Gordon's favorite. Use it for a chopped salad with chicken, beets, and crumbled blue cheese, or have it with a plain green salad of Romaine lettuce.

Every Saturday night you'll find me glued to the television set watching "X Factor" (our version of "American Idol") and eating chips—my biggest weakness. The recipes for dips I give in this chapter are what I eat on the side. If you want to be more virtuous than me, have crudités or ciabatta toasts instead of chips!

There's never an excuse for serving store-bought gravy. If you've gone to the trouble of selecting wonderful meat that has been farmed with care and properly butchered, my Homemade Gravy is what it deserves (*see* page 282). It's fairly hands off and not much effort to make—all you really need to remember is to keep scraping the pan.

Try to get into the habit of making Tomato Sauce (*see* page 278) in bulk, so you can store it. It's rich and deliciously easy, and you will feel so satisfied afterward. The best thing is that most of the ingredients come from the pantry, so you will never be at a loss.

Tomato & tarragon mayonnaise

You really need a food processor or immersion blender to prepare easily. There are big pieces of tomato here as it's quite a rustic recipe. If you want something more refined, simply cut the tomatoes smaller. This is great with cold chicken or when used to dress a potato salad.

Makes about 1⅓ cups
Preparation time 10 minutes
Can be made in advance

½ cup olive oil
1¾ cups vegetable oil
3 egg yolks
1 tbsp white wine vinegar
1 tsp dry mustard
2 tsp chopped tarragon
15 cherry tomatoes, quartered
juice of ½ lemon (about 1½ tbsp)
sea salt and black pepper

1 Pour the oils into a large measuring cup.

2 Put the eggs, vinegar, and mustard into the bowl of a food processor and blend for 20 seconds, then slowly drizzle in the oils (*see* secret, below). As the mixture starts to thicken (you will hear the blade begin to make a different noise) pour the oil in a little faster.

3 When the mayonnaise is the right consistency, transfer it to a large bowl. Fold in the tarragon and tomatoes, followed by the lemon juice and salt and pepper. Keep in a sealed jar or covered bowl in the refrigerator for up to 2 days.

How to make mayonnaise

Don't be alarmed at the thought of making mayonnaise; it's really not difficult. The only trick is the speed at which you add the oil to room-temperature egg yolks. It needs to be poured in very slowly and patiently—literally drop by drop at first—while you whisk or process continuously to create an emulsion. You will see the sauce coming together. If it splits, start again with new egg yolks.

Chile & lime mayonnaise

This is the perfect accompaniment to shrimp, giving a new twist to a shrimp cocktail. You can vary this recipe, omitting the chile if serving it to children, or using lemon instead of lime. It will still be utterly delicious!

Serves 6–8
Preparation time 5 minutes
Can be made in advance

½ tsp red pepper flakes
2 egg yolks
juice of 1 lime (about 2 tbsp)
sea salt and black pepper
1¼ cups plus 1 tsp vegetable oil

1 Put the pepper flakes, egg yolks, lime juice, salt, and pepper in the container that fits your hand-held electric mixer, or into a food processor. Blend together until frothy.

2 Gradually add the oil (*see* secret, page 272). The mayonnaise should be thick and glossy. If it is too thick, beat in a splash of water.

Cheese dip

My biggest weakness in life is chips and dip in front of the television on Saturday nights with the family. If you want a healthier option, try this dip alongside a platter of carrot and celery sticks, pieces of sweet pepper, and crusty bread.

Serves 6–8
Preparation time 5 minutes
Can be made in advance

10½oz soft goat cheese (chèvre)
3½oz cream cheese
4 tbsp heavy cream
3 tsp truffle oil (optional)
2 tbsp snipped chives
sea salt and black pepper

1 Simply mix together the cheeses then add the cream and truffle oil (if using). Finish by stirring in the chives and seasoning with salt and pepper.

Don't be afraid of goat cheese

I've lost count of how often I've heard friends say they don't like goat cheese, and how many of the same people love this dip! These days, mild, creamy goat cheese logs are as mellow as any other soft cheese and just as useful. I find that children love it and, of course, it's excellent for those with an intolerance to cows' milk. Keep the stronger-flavored, hard goat cheese for aficionados.

yum

Jessica

Creamy mustard vinaigrette

This is the perfect dressing for a chunky dish such as mixed bean salad, as the creaminess coats the beans. It's versatile and great poured over almost any salad, so it's good to have a jar in the refrigerator to be used at any time.

Makes about ¾ cup
Preparation time 5 minutes
Can be made in advance

6 tbsp olive oil
2 tbsp white wine vinegar
2 tbsp grainy mustard
2 tbsp crème fraîche
sea salt and black pepper

1 Place all the dressing ingredients into a pitcher—or pour them into a clean lidded glass jar—and whisk briskly (or shake the jar) until the vinaigrette has a smooth, creamy appearance. Taste and adjust the seasoning, making sure the balance of flavors is as you like it; you can add more of any ingredient to suit your palate. Store the vinaigrette in the refrigerator until needed.

2 Always leave it until the last moment before dressing a salad, and give the vinaigrette a final whisk or shake before pouring.

How to make the perfect vinaigrette

Vinaigrette combines oil and vinegar to give a smooth, emulsified dressing. In this recipe I have used grainy mustard as this helps the emulsion to hold. The crème fraîche gives a creamy finish. Remember to season dressings with salt and pepper as this will bring out their taste. Store in the refrigerator until needed, although I would use it within 2 days.

Homemade ranch-style dressing

Use different herbs from those suggested below to suit your taste, or scallions for a bit of crunch. This dressing works well for salads, as a dipping sauce, or with baked potatoes. As a family, we all have different favorite salad dressings, but this manages to appeal to all of us.

Serves 6–8
Preparation time 5 minutes
Can be made in advance

½ cup mayonnaise
½ cup sour cream
½ cup buttermilk
1 tbsp snipped chives
1 tsp finely chopped parsley leaves
1 tsp finely chopped dill fronds
1 garlic clove, crushed
sea salt and black pepper

1 Simply mix all the ingredients together really well, season to taste with salt and pepper and serve at room temperature.

Buttermilk: the secret weapon

It's always worth having a container of tangy, yogurty buttermilk in the refrigerator as it has so many uses. You will find it in most larger supermarkets. As well as giving a flavor boost to my dressing recipe here, it can act as a raising agent in yeast-free baking, such as for Irish soda bread or scones. Its slight acidity also makes it a valuable ingredient in marinades for chicken, where it acts as a tenderizer.

Tomato sauce

This is great for pasta sauces or pizza toppings. Make a large batch and cook it slowly until it begins to thicken and its flavors intensify, filling the house with a lovely aroma. This is a base sauce, so it's very adaptable; try adding pancetta, marinated peppers, or mushrooms.

Makes 5 cups
Preparation time 10 minutes
Cooking time 30 minutes
Can be made in advance
Suitable for freezing

drizzle of olive oil
2 red onions, finely sliced
2 garlic cloves, finely sliced
¾ cup red wine
3 × 14.5oz cans peeled cherry tomatoes
generous splash of Worcestershire sauce
handful of basil leaves, roughly chopped
sea salt and black pepper

1 Pour the olive oil into a large pan and place over a medium heat. When it's hot, add the onions and garlic and gently fry for 3–4 minutes, until softened. Add the red wine and allow to reduce for a few minutes until the liquid has almost evaporated.

2 Pour in the tomatoes and heat through, then add the Worcestershire sauce and basil and bring to a simmer. Bubble gently for 20–25 minutes, or until the sauce starts to thicken.

3 Season with salt and pepper to taste, then allow to cool completely before refrigerating.

Tomato salsa

Again, I have this on my chips! But this is a far more versatile recipe and is fabulous with cold chicken, alongside any salad, or used as a topping over a crunchy bruschetta (see page 200). All in all, a very useful thing to have stashed away in the refrigerator.

Serves 6–8
Preparation time 10 minutes
Can be made in advance

2 cups ripe on-the-vine tomatoes, quartered
3 tbsp olive oil
1 red chile, seeded and finely chopped
1 small red onion, finely chopped
3 scallions, finely chopped
2 tbsp balsamic vinegar
1 tsp sesame oil
1 tbsp finely chopped cilantro or basil
sea salt

1 Mix together all the ingredients and season with salt. Chill in the refrigerator until ready to serve.

How to choose the best tomatoes

Always keep a look out for the reddest, most plump and aromatic fruits you can find. The ripest tomatoes are often revealed by their lovely herbal scent. Go for tomatoes that are blemish- and bruise-free and have a little "give" when lightly pressed.

Creamy corn salsa

This makes a nice accompaniment to cold meats, especially ham and salami, or cheese and potatoes, either hot or cold. It's always an indispensable part of a family lunch of leftovers, with lots of salads on the table for us all to help ourselves.

Serves 6–8
Preparation time 5 minutes
Can be made in advance

11oz can sweet corn, drained
1 red chile, seeded and finely chopped
2 ripe plum tomatoes, cut into ½in dice
1 garlic clove, finely chopped
juice of ½ lime (about 1 tbsp)
1 tbsp maple syrup
2 tbsp sour cream
sea salt and black pepper
1 tbsp finely chopped cilantro leaves

1 Mix together all the ingredients and allow the flavors to fuse in the refrigerator until ready to use.

The best fresh sweet corn
For this dish, I have used canned sweet corn. However, if you choose fresh corn, make sure you select plump-looking ears, with bright green, stiff husks, and no sign of dry or shriveled kernels. Remove the husks, pull away all the "silk" (the hairs you will find inside) and carefully cut down the cob lengthwise to remove the kernels, using a sharp knife. Rinse. Use the kernels as soon as possible, so they retain the maximum sweetness. Cook them in a pan of water for 2–3 minutes, or until tender, then drain. If you are not using all the kernels, you can easily freeze them for use later.

Chunky apple sauce

I use Braeburn apples to give a textured sauce as they don't break down into a mush. They have a lovely sweet yet tangy taste that is a wonderful accompaniment to my Crackling Roast Pork (see page 27). If you prefer a smoother sauce, try Granny Smith apples instead.

Serves 6
Preparation time 10 minutes
Cooking time 20–25 minutes
Can be made in advance

6 Braeburn apples
small knob of butter (1–2 tbsp)
squeeze of lemon juice
1 tbsp sugar
splash of water

1 Peel and core the apples and cut into ½in cubes. Place them in a pan with the butter, then cook immediately over medium heat (*see* secret, below).

2 Cook the apples for 20–25 minutes, stirring frequently, until softened. Add the lemon juice and sugar and a splash or two of cold water, until you have the consistency you like.

Preventing discoloration

It is important to begin to cook apples as soon as they are prepared, or they will begin to oxidize and turn an unpleasant brown color. To keep apples beautifully white in a fruit salad, toss them in lemon juice immediately after cutting. This will protect the slices from discoloration. The same applies to avocado in guacamole recipes (try lime to preserve the color), or the cut edges of fresh artichokes.

Homemade gravy

The most important thing to remember for excellent gravy is to let the meat catch very slightly on the base of the roasting pan, so you can scrape up all the sticky, deeply savory bits into the sauce. Don't let it burn, though, or it will be too bitter to serve.

Makes about 3 cups
Preparation time 10 minutes
Cooking time 1 hour 15 minutes
Can be made in advance
Suitable for freezing

2lb 4oz chicken wings
1 tbsp tomato puree
6 garlic cloves, skin on, crushed
1 onion, roughly chopped
3 thyme sprigs
3½ cups white wine
4 cups chicken stock (*see* page 37)
sea salt and black pepper

1 Preheat the oven to 375°F.

2 Place the chicken wings in a flameproof roasting dish or heavy roasting pan and cook for 45–50 minutes, or until golden brown. Remove the chicken from the dish then transfer the dish to the stovetop over medium heat.

3 Stir the tomato puree, garlic, and onion into the chicken juices in the dish, scraping the chicken bits off the bottom. Add the thyme, wine, and stock. Increase the heat and bring to a boil, continuing to scrape all the lovely browned bits from the base of the dish (this is where the flavor is). Let the gravy reduce for 15–20 minutes.

4 Give the gravy a final scrape, then pass it through a fine-mesh strainer. Taste and season with salt and pepper, then. If you would like a thicker consistency, boil down a little further.

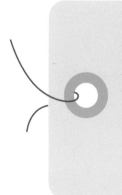

Gravy tricks

Any piece of meat large enough to roast will give plenty of excellent gravy, especially if cooked on a bed of root vegetables. Add red wine or water to beef juices; red or white wine or stock to lamb; wine, cider, or apple juice to pork; white wine to chicken. Always scrape in the bits from the base of the pan, then reduce the liquid by half. For thicker gravy you may need to stir in flour before the liquid.

Index

almonds
cherry and almond loaf 248
plum and almond pudding 228
anchovies
anchovy, tomato, and bacon pasta
sauce 107
chicken cacciatore 34
curly kale with anchovies, onion, and
garlic 176
perfect pizza 198
pissaladière 132
sirloin steak flavoured with anchovy
and garlic 60
apples
apple and raspberry crumb muffins 257
chunky apple sauce 280
apricots 226
apricot, raspberry, and ginger
crumble 226
artichokes
ricotta, pepper, and artichoke
quiche 130
arugula
chicken, lemon, and arugula risotto 115
arugula salad 59
asparagus 182
haddock and spring vegetable
risotto 112
asparagus soup 182

bacon
anchovy, tomato, and bacon pasta
sauce 107
bacon, mushroom, and cheese pastry
parcels 127
fresh green salad with bacon 185
pasta with bacon and vegetable
sauce 108
baked beans 11
barbecuing sweet corn 178
bean sprouts 174
peapod salad 174
beef
beef and eggplant rigatoni bake with
tomato and basil 104
sirloin steak flavoured with anchovy
and garlic 60
spicy beef stew 30
stock 37
beer, mussels with Belgian 98
beets, roasted with crème fraîche and
chives 169
blackberry ice cream 212
blanching vegetables 170
bowls 8
bread 192
easy handmade white bread 194
tomato and prosciutto bruschetta 200
bread crumbs 143
bread crumb coatings 89

breakfast rolls 134
broccoli
pork chops with honey and mustard
glaze 54
broth, chicken 37
bruschetta 192
tomato and prosciutto bruschetta 200
burgers, shaping 24
butter frosting 246, 254
buttermilk
homemade ranch-style dressing 277
butternut squash
Thai red curry 92
turkey scallops with mashed
butternut squash and corn 66

cake pans 8
lining 248
cakes 241–55
cherry and almond loaf 248
chocolate heaven cupcakes 254
creaming batter 246
cupcake party time 250
folding in flour 254
storing 242
testing for doneness 244
Victoria sponge 246
calamari
preparation 96
sautéed calamari with chorizo and
peppers 96
caramel 145
caramelized peaches with hazelnut
crème fraîche 224
carrot and raisin cupcakes 260
casseroles *see* stews
cauliflower cheese my way 158
celery soup 184
Champagne cocktail 238
cheese
bacon, mushroom, and cheese pastry
parcels 127
beef and eggplant rigatoni bake with
tomato and basil 104
breaded veal scallops with mozzarella
and tomato and red pepper
sauce 58–9
cauliflower cheese my way 158
cheese dip 274
cheese sauce 158
cream cheese fava beans and peas 172
Parmesan chicken drumsticks 32
ricotta, pepper, and artichoke
quiche 130
cheese shavers 8
cheesecake, chocolate 236
cherries
cherry and almond loaf 248
cherry and chocolate mousse 233
fresh cherry jam tart 148

chicken 34
chicken, lemon, and arugula
risotto 115
chicken broth 37
chicken cacciatore 34
free-range chicken 38
homemade gravy 282
Parmesan chicken drumsticks 32
poached whole chicken 38
spicy chicken wings 62
stock 37
chiles 186
chile and lime mayonnaise 274
napa cabbage and chile salad 186
Chinese duck breast wraps 64
chocolate
cherry and chocolate mousse 233
chocolate, fruit, and nut cookies 262
chocolate cheesecake 236
chocolate heaven cupcakes 254
melting 233
chopping boards 8
chops 44
chorizo
sautéed calamari with chorizo and
peppers 96
shrimp, chorizo, and baby zucchini
tempura 135
Spanish fish soup 75
coatings
bread crumb coatings 89
for meat 32
cocktail, simple Champagne 238
coconut milk 214
coconut sorbets 214
Lauren's meatballs 24
Thai red curry 92
cod 79
cookie cutters 8
cookies 242
chocolate, fruit, and nut cookies 262
Garibaldi cookies 256
gingerbread men and hearts 266
lemon and thyme shortbread 264
storing 242
corn
barbecuing 178
pan-fried corn 178
turkey scallops with mashed
butternut squash and corn 66
see also sweet corn
couscous 102
healthy couscous, my style 118
preparation 118
crab
crab and sweet corn soup 95
preparation 95
crackling roast pork 27
cream
Eton mess 210

crème fraîche, hazelnut 224
crumbles 206, 257
    apricot, raspberry, and ginger
        crumble 226
cupcake party time 250
curly kale with anchovies, onion, and
    garlic 176
currants
    Garibaldi cookies 256
curry paste
    Lauren's meatballs 24
    Thai red curry 92
    turkey masala kebabs 67

deep-frying 122, 135
dip, cheese 274
dorade, salt-baked 82
dough 192–6
dressings 270
    homemade ranch-style dressing 277
duck
    Chinese duck breast wraps 64
    marinated duck breasts 63
    preparing breasts 63

eggplants
    beef and eggplant rigatoni bake with
        tomato and basil 104
    Lauren's meatballs 24
    pasta with bacon and vegetable
        sauce 108
equipment 8
Eton mess 210

fava beans
    cream cheese fava beans and peas 172
    double-podding 172
fish 69–99
    bread crumb coatings 89
    cooking with pasta 110
    marinating 72
    poaching liquid 112
    pork with 75
    skinning 74
    sustainable fish 79
    see also monkfish, salmon etc
fish cakes, smoked haddock 88–9
food processors 8
free-range chicken 38
freezers 11, 216
fries, best-ever homemade 164
frosting
    butter frosting 246, 254
frozen fruit 221
fruit 206
    frozen fruit 221
    impressively pretty fruit tarts 138
    see also apples, strawberries etc

Garibaldi cookies 256

garlic
    grating on toast 200
    roasted guinea fowl with lemon and
        garlic 40
ginger
    gingerbread men and hearts 266
    homemade ginger lemonade 232
    pear and ginger steamed sponge
        pudding 229
glaze icing 250
goat cheese
    cheese dip 274
grapes
    frozen fruit 221
graters, microplane 8
gravy 270, 282
green beans with lemon and
    pancetta 170
green salad with bacon 185
ground meat 48
guinea fowl with lemon and garlic 40

haddock *see* **smoked haddock**
ham hock pot pie 124
hazelnuts
    chocolate, fruit, and nut cookies 262
    hazelnut crème fraîche 224
herbs, roasting with 166
honey 168
    honey and thyme roasted turnips 168
hot sauce 11

ice cream 206, 212, 217
    blackberry ice cream 212
icing
    glaze icing 250
Indian lamb chops 46
ingredients 11

jointing poultry 40

kale 176
    curly kale with anchovies, onion, and
        garlic 176
kebabs 44
    broiled tuna and vegetable kebabs 85
    turkey masala kebabs 67
kidneys
    lamb kidneys in cream and mushroom
        sauce 50
    trimming 50
kitchen towels 8
knife sharpeners 8
knives 8
koftas, shaping 24

lamb 44
    homemade lamb sausages in
        prosciutto 48
    Indian lamb chops 46

    Lauren's meatballs 24
    really rustic shoulder of lamb 16
    shepherd's pie 20
lamb kidneys in cream and mushroom
    sauce 50
Lauren's meatballs 24
lemon 232
    homemade ginger lemonade 232
    lemon and thyme shortbread 264
    phyllo lemon tart 150
    raspberry and lemon *torta* 244
    roasted guinea fowl with lemon and
        garlic 40
lentils 163
    tarka dal 163
lime
    chile and lime mayonnaise 274
liquid, poaching fish 112

mangos 223
    mango and passion fruit dessert 223
marinades
    for fish 72
    for meat 62
    using yogurt 46
mashing potatoes 20
mayonnaise 270
    chile and lime mayonnaise 274
    homemade ranch-style dressing 277
    tomato and tarragon mayonnaise 272
meat
    browning 30
    coatings 32, 89
    gravy 282
    heat and 64
    marinating 62
    preparing scallops 66
    preparing for roasting 27
    quick and easy recipes 43–67
    slow cooking 13–41
    yogurt marinades 46
    see also beef, lamb etc
meatballs
    Lauren's 24
    shaping 24
melon cooler 218
meringues 208
    Eton mess 210
microplane graters 8
miso 86
    seared coriander-crusted tuna steaks
        with miso 86
mixing bowls 8
monkfish
    Moroccan fish tagine 72
mousse, cherry and chocolate 233
muffins 242
    apple and raspberry crumb muffins 257
    carrot and raisin cupcakes 260
    muffin cases 260

mushrooms
    bacon, mushroom, and cheese pastry
        parcels 127
    cleaning 180
    lamb kidneys in cream and mushroom
        sauce 50
    pasta with bacon and vegetable
        sauce 108
    stuffed mushrooms 180
    turkey masala kebabs 67
mussels
    mussels with Belgian beer 98
    preparation 98
mustard vinaigrette 276

napa cabbage and chile salad 186
noodles
    seared coriander-crusted tuna steaks
        with miso 86
nuts, toasting 224

offal 44
oil 11
olive oil 8
olives
    pissaladière 132
orange sorbet 216
oven mitts 8

pancetta
    anchovy, tomato, and bacon pasta
        sauce 107
    breakfast rolls 134
    green beans with lemon and
        pancetta 170
    pork loin with pancetta and sage 51
pans 8
Parmesan chicken drumsticks 32
parsnips, rosemary roasted 166
passion fruit
    mango and passion fruit dessert 223
    simple Champagne cocktail 238
pasta 102
    anchovy, tomato, and bacon pasta
        sauce 107
    beef and eggplant rigatoni bake with
        tomato and basil 104
    cooking 107
    cooking fish with 110
    fresh vs dried 108
    pasta with bacon and vegetable
        sauce 108
    shapes 104
    simple salmon, dill, and crème fraîche
        pasta 110
pastries
    breakfast rolls 134
pastry
    covering pie dishes 124
    pastry shells 142

phyllo dough 150
    rolling out 132
    sweet shortcrust pastry 142
pastry cream 141
peaches
    caramelized peaches with hazelnut
        crème fraîche 224
peapod salad 174
pear and ginger steamed sponge
    pudding 229
peas
    cream cheese fava beans and peas 172
phyllo dough 150
phyllo lemon tart 150
pies 122
    bacon, mushroom, and cheese pastry
        parcels 127
    classic ham hock pot pie 124
    covering 124
    pollack and shrimp pie with smoked
        paprika mashed potato topping 78–9
    shepherd's pie 20
pineapple 222
    frozen fruit 221
    pineapple tarte tatin 145
    pineapple with a lime twist 222
pissaladière 132
pizza 192, 196
    perfect pizza 198
plum and almond pudding 228
poaching liquid, fish 112
pollack and shrimp pie with smoked
    paprika mashed potato topping 78–9
pork
    crackling roast pork 27
    pork chops with honey and mustard
        glaze 54
    pork loin with pancetta and sage 51
    preparing chops 54
    simple pork stir-fry 56
    tenderloin 51
    with fish 75
potatoes
    baked potatoes 160
    best-ever homemade fries 164
    filled potato skins 160
    mashing 20
    new potato salad with crème fraîche
        and cilantro 188
    pollack and shrimp pie with smoked
        paprika mashed potato topping 78–9
    roasted guinea fowl with lemon and
        garlic 40
    shepherd's pie 20
    smoked haddock fish cakes 88–9
poultry
    jointing 40
    see also chicken, duck etc
shrimp
    shrimp, chorizo, and baby zucchini

tempura 135
    pollack and shrimp pie with smoked
        paprika mashed potato topping 78–9
    preparation 92
    red rice salad 116
    Thai red curry 92
prosciutto
    homemade lamb sausages in
        prosciutto 48
    tomato and prosciutto bruschetta 200
puff pastry rims, tarts 148

quiche, ricotta, pepper, and artichoke 130

raisins
    carrot and raisin cupcakes 260
    chocolate, fruit, and nut cookies 262
ranch-style dressing 277
raspberries
    apple and raspberry crumb muffins 257
    apricot, raspberry, and ginger
        crumble 226
    raspberry and lemon *torta* 244
    raspberry sorbet 217
red rice salad 116
refrigerators 11
rice
    cooking 116
    red rice salad 116
    steamed rice 92
    see also risotto
ricotta, pepper, and artichoke quiche 130
rigatoni bake, beef and eggplant with
    tomato and basil 104
risotto 102, 115
    chicken, lemon, and arugula risotto 115
    haddock and spring vegetable
        risotto 112
roasting
    preparing meat 27
    vegetables 169
    with herbs 166

salads
    arugula salad 59
    dressing 185
    fresh green salad with bacon 185
    healthy couscous, my style 118
    napa cabbage and chile salad 186
    new potato salad with crème fraîche
        and cilantro 188
    peapod salad 174
    red rice salad 116
    salmon
    salmon fillet in black sauce 74
    simple salmon, dill, and crème fraîche
        pasta 110
salsas
    creamy corn salsa 279
    tomato salsa 278

salt-baked dorade 82
sauces 270
    anchovy, tomato, and bacon pasta
        sauce 107
    cheese sauce 158
    chunky apple sauce 280
    homemade gravy 282
    tomato sauce 278
sausages
    breakfast rolls 134
    homemade lamb sausages in
        prosciutto 48
    see also chorizo
scales 8
scallops, preparing 66
scissors 8
scones 202
shellfish 70
    see also crab, mussels etc
shepherd's pie 20
shortbread, lemon and thyme 264
sirloin steak flavoured with anchovy and
    garlic 60
skinning fish 74
slow cooking meat 13–41
smoked haddock
    haddock and spring vegetable
        risotto 112
    smoked haddock fish cakes 88–9
sorbets 206, 217
    coconut 214
    orange 216
    raspberry 217
soups 184
    asparagus soup 182
    celery soup 184
    chicken broth 37
    crab and sweet corn soup 95
    seared coriander-crusted tuna steaks
        with miso 86
    Spanish fish soup 75
spaghetti
    pasta with bacon and vegetable
        sauce 108
    simple salmon, dill, and crème fraîche
        pasta 110
Spanish fish soup 75
spatulas, plastic 8
spices 11, 266
spicy beef stew 30
sprinkles 11
squash see butternut squash
squid
    preparation 96
    sautéed calamari with chorizo and
        peppers 96
steak see beef
steamed sponge pudding, pear and
    ginger 229
stews

chicken cacciatore 34
    spicy beef stew 30
stir-fries 44, 56
    simple pork stir-fry 56
stock 37
storing cakes and biscuits 242
strainers 8
strawberries
    Eton mess 210
sugar
    brown sugar 236
    caramel 145
sweet peppers
    breaded veal scallops with mozzarella
        and tomato and red pepper
        sauce 58–9
    broiled tuna and vegetable kebabs 85
    Moroccan fish tagine 72
    ricotta, pepper, and artichoke
        quiche 130
    sautéed calamari with chorizo and
        peppers 96
    simple pork stir-fry 56
    Spanish fish soup 75
    turkey masala kebabs 67
sweet corn
    crab and sweet corn soup 95
    creamy corn salsa 279
    see also corn
sweet shortcrust pastry 142

tagine, Moroccan fish 72
tagliatelle
    anchovy, tomato, and bacon pasta
        sauce 107
tarka dal 163
tarts 138
    fresh cherry jam tart 148
    impressively pretty fruit tarts 138
    phyllo lemon tart 150
    pineapple tarte tatin 145
    pissaladière 132
    puff pastry rims 148
    traditional treacle tart 143
tempura, shrimp, chorizo, and baby
    zucchini 135
Thai red curry 92
toast, grating garlic on 200
toasting nuts 224
tomatoes 278
    anchovy, tomato, and bacon pasta
        sauce 107
    beef and eggplant rigatoni bake with
        tomato and basil 104
    breaded veal scallops with mozzarella
        and tomato and red pepper
        sauce 58–9
    chicken cacciatore 34
    Chinese duck breast wraps 64
    pasta with bacon and vegetable

sauce 108
    perfect pizza 198
    spicy beef stew 30
    Thai red curry 92
    tomato and prosciutto bruschetta 200
    tomato and tarragon mayonnaise 272
    tomato salsa 278
    tomato sauce 278
torta, raspberry and lemon 244
treacle tart 143
tuna 85
    broiled tuna and vegetable kebabs 85
    seared coriander-crusted tuna steaks
        with miso 86
turkey
    diced turkey 67
    preparing scallops 66
    turkey scallops with mashed
        butternut squash and corn 66
    turkey masala kebabs 67
turnips, honey and thyme roasted 168
turnovers 127

veal 59
    breaded veal scallops with mozzarella
        and tomato and red pepper
        sauce 58–9
vegetables 11, 153–89
    blanching 170
    chicken broth 37
    roasting 169
    stir-fries 56
    see also eggplants, tomatoes etc
Victoria sponge 246
vinaigrette, creamy mustard 276

whiting
    Spanish fish soup 75

yeast 196
yogurt
    Indian lamb chops 46
    meat marinades 46
    melon cooler 218

zucchini
    haddock and spring vegetable
        risotto 112
    shrimp, chorizo, and baby zucchini
tempura 135
    stuffed zucchini 156

To Gordon, Megan, Jack, Holly, and Matilda, the best team x

THANKS

I would like to thank so many people for so much help, support, and fun with this book.

Karen Taylor, so incredibly organized, efficient and calm throughout—having three sons, she is not phased by anything! Thanks also to Chris Taylor, for all his help and hard work, along with stories of his rock band to entertain... Lisa Harrison for helping with recipe testing—having your eagle eye over my recipes is very comforting! Paula, Pene, and Sarah, the shoots all ran so smoothly and everything looks so beautiful with all your creative inputs, thank you. Laura, I love all your photos, the recipes look amazing, the colors vibrant and fun.

Thanks also to Lucy Bannell—I have a huge amount of admiration for you working and turning things around at the speed you do with baby twins; you make it look effortless! I am still trying to figure it out and my twins are ten!

Thanks to Leanne Bryan, for ensuring the detail is just right, and to Becca Spry for putting together such a lovely team for me to work with and making it such an enjoyable project; I have loved every minute and having you there for ideas and banter has been brilliant.

Lastly, thanks to Martine Carter, for bringing it all together.

Tana Ramsay

Tana's Kitchen Secrets
by Tana Ramsay

First published in Great Britain in 2010 by Mitchell Beazley, an imprint of Octopus Publishing Group Limited, Endeavour House, 189 Shaftesbury Avenue, London, WC2H 8JG
www.octopusbooks.co.uk

An Hachette UK Company
www.hachette.co.uk

Distributed in the United States and Canada by Hachette Book Group USA, 237 Park Avenue, New York, NY 10017 USA

ISBN: 978 1 84533 550 2

Set in Berling LT and Justlefthand

Printed and bound in China

Commissioning Editor Becca Spry
Senior Editor Leanne Bryan
Art Director Pene Parker
Senior Art Editor Juliette Norsworthy
Designer Paula Macfarlane
Copy-editor Lucy Bannell
Photographer Laura Hynd
Home Economists Lisa Harrison, Karen Taylor, Robert Allison and Chris Taylor
Stylist Sarah O'Keefe
Americanizer Marisa Bulzone
Proofreader Nicole Foster
Indexer Hilary Bird
Production Manager Peter Hunt

With thanks to:

Summerill & Bishop
100 Portland Road,
London, W11 4LQ
tel: 020 7727 1322
www.summerillandbishop.com

Ceramica Blue
10 Blenheim Crescent,
London, W11 1NN
tel: 020 7727 0288
email: shop@ceramicablue.co.uk
www.ceramicablue.co.uk